SpringerBriefs in Finance

More information about this series at http://www.springer.com/series/10282

Mathias Schmidt

Pricing and Liquidity of Complex and Structured Derivatives

Deviation of a Risk Benchmark Based on Credit and Option Market Data

Springer

Mathias Schmidt
Hamburg
Germany

This book is based on a dissertation at the WHU – Otto Beisheim School of Management at the chair of Empirical Capital Market Research under the title "Pricing and Liquidity of Complex and Structured Derivatives".

ISSN 2193-1720 ISSN 2193-1739 (electronic)
SpringerBriefs in Finance
ISBN 978-3-319-45969-1 ISBN 978-3-319-45970-7 (eBook)
DOI 10.1007/978-3-319-45970-7

Library of Congress Control Number: 2016950744

Printed on acid-free paper

This Springer imprint is published by Springer Nature
The registered company is Springer International Publishing AG
The registered company address is: Gewerbestrasse 11, 6330 Cham, Switzerland

Acknowledgement

I am using this opportunity to express my gratitude to everyone who supported me throughout the course of this Ph.D. project.

Firstly, I would like to sincerely thank my superadvisor Prof. Lutz Johanning for the continuous support of my Ph.D. study and related research, for his knowledge and guidance.

Besides my superadvisor, I would like to thank Prof. Burcin Yurtoglu for dedicating his time and work to the assessment of this thesis.

I would also like to thank my parents in law for their great support and help in many ways throughout writing this thesis. I am deeply sad, that my late father-in law has not seen my thesis being published in this book.

I especially want to thank my parents for their enduring and loving support through my whole academic career, which climaxed in the Ph.D. thesis. All this would not have been possible without you.

At the end I would like express gratitude to my beloved wife Anna for spending countless hours with me on this thesis and for all of the sacrifices that she has made on my behalf. Words cannot express how grateful I am for your support especially in difficult times.

Contents

Abbreviations

ATM	At-the-money (meaning options with the strike equal to the spot price)
BPS	Basis points (100 bps = 1 %)
CDS	Credit default swap
DC	Credit derivative determination committee (ISDA)
DOOM	Deep out-of-the-money
DTCC	Depository Trust & Clearing Corporation
ECB	European Central Bank
EOD	End of day
ISDA	International swaps and derivate association
KMV	Kealhofer, Merton and Vasicek (model)
OIS	Overnight index swap
OTC	Over-the-counter (meaning not exchange-traded)
PD	Probability of default
R	Recovery rate
SOD	Strike of default
TMT	Technology, media and telecommunication
TTM	Time to maturity (denoted in years)
URC	Unit recovery claims

List of Figures

List of Tables

Chapter 1
Introduction

In this dissertation, we discuss several aspects concerning Credit Default Swaps (CDS) such as pricing methods and the market liquidity of CDS contracts. In a CDS contract, the protection seller secures the protection buyer, sometimes called the investor, against a credit event of the reference entity. The reference entity or underlying can be a corporation or a country. On the financial market we also find CDS indices, which consist of CDS contracts with either companies or countries as underlying. There are mainly four different applications for CDS products. First, CDS contracts can be used to dispose of the credit risk concerning a certain reference entity. For example, if company A offers company B a credit, company A can secure itself against the default of company B by buying a CDS concerning company B from company C. Secondly, investors can apply CDS products for speculative reasons. If the investor believes the CDS spread is too high or too low, the investor can create a basis trade, which is a combination of CDS, cash bond and interest rate swap, in order to speculate yields. Third, the CDS investor can gain arbitrage, if the bond coupon is higher than the CDS coupon. Last, CDS products can help to diversify a credit portfolio and to reduce concentration of risk. For example, if one credit with an extraordinary nominal exists in a credit portfolio, the portfolio manager can invest in a CDS protection on this particular underlying and sell a CDS protection on an underlying, which so far does not exist in the portfolio. The concentration of risk is thereby reduced and the credit risk of the portfolio is further diversified.

Blythe Masters from J.P. Morgan & Co. invented the CDS contract in 1994 and the market for CDS has grown extraordinarily since its inception. In 1998, approximately 300 billion US dollars were invested in CDS contracts and the market increased until reaching its peak at the end of 2007, with an investment sum of approximately 62 trillion US dollars. During the financial crises of 2007 and the following years, the market was distressed and has still not completely recovered since. However, today CDS products are still very important tools in the market. For example, between April and May 2012 JPMorgan Chase & Co., who is known as one of the top CDS trading banks worldwide, lost about two billion US dollars

M. Schmidt, *Pricing and Liquidity of Complex and Structured Derivatives*,
SpringerBriefs in Finance, DOI 10.1007/978-3-319-45970-7_1

within a few weeks as a result of speculative CDS trading. Not only since the financial crises of 2007 has there been an ambition to imply market standards in the CDS market. Until 2009 CDS contracts were only over-the-counter (OTC) products, meaning they were not exchange-listed transactions. Therefore, the International Swaps and Derivate Association (ISDA) set up some standards for CDS contracts. The ISDA was found in 1985 and is a global trade organisation with the goal of making OTC transactions safe and efficient. Today the ISDA has over 850 members, which are all participants in the financial markets, in over 67 countries. Due to these ISDA standards, the liquidity, the transparency and the comparability of CDS transaction has increased. Further, the usage of a central clearinghouse has diminished the counterparty risk and reduced the OTC characterisation of CDS trades. Nowadays, nearly 90 % of all CDS trades worldwide are cleared and settled by the Depository Trust & Clearing Corporation (DTCC). With the "big bang protocol" in the US and the "small bang protocol" in Europe in 2009, the ISDA implemented the credit derivative determination committee (DC), which has the power to decide in challenging cases whether a credit event occurred or not. The DC also determines the procedure with CDS contracts in case of a merger, acquisition or a split of the reference corporation. All that being said, CDS products are a very good alternative to standard insurances. Additionally, CDS products grant a high level of transparency and a high degree of liquidity especially to standard insurance products. Even though the ISDA set up CDS standards, market participants are still able to construct tailor-made CDS contracts to their particular needs.

One effect of the financial crises has been the change in the shape, structure and deviation of interest rate curves. Due to the lack of liquidity in the market and a growing mistrust towards other financial institutes or companies, the interest rate curves are no longer strictly increasing. In particular, a big difference between the three and the six months tenors for interest rate swaps rose due to a higher default risk of the counterparty. Further, the European Central Bank (ECB) decreased the interest rate to a historical low level of 0.25 % in November 2013 in order to cope with the consequences of the still continuing crises of the international financial markets. The aim of the ECB is to flood the market with liquidity, because this significant lack of the liquidity during the financial crisis has been observed before. All interest rate curves dropped tremendously as a result of the ECB lowering interest rates. Even though the markets are partly recovering from the financial crises, the ECB remains set on keeping the interest rate down in order to prevent a deflation and to enable companies to cheaply borrow money from banks, especially in countries that suffered tremendously under the financial crisis such as Greece, Spain and Portugal. On June 11, 2014, the current president of the ECB, Mario Draghi, announced that interest rates will drop again. Consequently, the ECB lowered the main refinancing operations rate to a level of 0.15 % and the deposit facility rate to a level of −0.10 %. This means that for the first time in the history of the ECB, it declared a negative deposit facility rate, meaning that it costs banks to deposit their money at the ECB. The aims of these actions were the reanimation of interbank market, the granting of credits to the retail market in the unstable countries in the Eurozone and resistance against deflation. The growth in the counterparty risk led to the need of a multi curve approach, where several interest rate curves are built for different tenor. Until the beginning of the financial crisis, the interest rate curves were nearly identical disregarding, which tenor was used. For example, an evaluation of a fix-to-floater interest rate swap with a variable tenor of three months and a fixed tenor of six months cannot be evaluated with one singular interest curve anymore. For the pricing of such an interest rate swap we need a discounting interest curve of the fixed and variable leg. Additionally, we require an interest rate curve of three months in order to calculate forward rates for the variable leg. Thus, the same interest rate curve cannot be applied to derive discount factors and forward rates. Therefore, the constructions of interest rate curves have become rather difficult as we briefly describe in this dissertation.

In the first paper of this quasi-cumulative dissertation, we outline several alternative methods of CDS pricing. The study of alternative pricing methods is to review whether more complex method are more exact than simpler ones. More complex methods take more time to implement and to run as well as they need more market data as input for their calculation. Therefore if simpler methods are suitable enough, the need for more sophisticated methods falls to the wayside. In general, there exist two different methods to evaluate a CDS. On the one hand, there is the structural approach, where balance sheets data are mandatory and the probability of default (PD) is modelled indirectly. The structural approach is based on the option pricing theory by Merton (1974) as well as Black and Scholes (1973). This approach assumes that the company's debt is similar to a bond and that the company's assets are of an option type. The company will default if the assets drop below the debts. Even though this approach is quite popular in the scientific world, it has several disadvantages. Probably the greatest disadvantage is its need for balance sheet data. Because up-to-date balance sheet data are rarely available, this approach makes it complicated to accurately evaluate CDS prices on any trading day. On the other hand, there is the reduced form approach, which is widely used by participants in the financial markets. This method is purely based on market data. We apply the reduced form method for the CDS pricing and examine three various minor models changes the standard evaluation. These following three approaches are (i) four different approaches to construct arbitrage-free survival respectively default probabilities, (ii) the influence of the different discounting rate curve and (iii) the handling of the CDS market data concerning their maturity. The iTraxx Europe is a CDS index existing of 125 CDS on European companies with an investment grade or higher. Since CDS indices have become very popular and possess a high degree of liquidity, we use this index as benchmark. We test their influence of the minor changes on historical data of the iTraxx Europe series 15 and its index members. For our empirical test of the different pricing approaches, we gathered all index market data as well as market data form the index members. Further, we examine whether the iTraxx index can be exactly reconstructed by all its members. Thus, we also test whether a lack of liquidity between the CDS index and the single-name CDS exists.

In the first paper we apply different input parameters to price CDS contracts using the reduced form approach. These approaches do not go far enough in terms of looking at CDS in a total different matter. If we compare CDS pricing methods, where mainly to different pricing methods exists, to the manifold pricing methods for options, we believe that there must be more potential in additional CDS pricing approaches. While we think about different perspectives on CDS contracts, there is one particular thought that we always took into consideration. From a protection seller's point of view the CDS is similar to a bond with the doubt of the nominal payment. We could even state that the payment in case of a credit event is somehow optional at the beginning of the contract. In case of a stock exchange listed company as the underlying of a CDS the protection seller would further like to know at which stock price the company might default. Thus, the CDS from a protection seller's view can be seen as an American digital option, if we assume the recovery rate to be known in advance, which is a standard assumption in the ISDA terms. Then the pay-off, in case of a credit event, is known and the credit event can occur at any time until maturity. These are the characteristics of an American digital option. From the reduced form approach for CDS pricing, we learn that we are able to derive the probability of default (PD) respectively the survival probability of the underlying from the CDS market spreads. However, these figures only represent credit market's view on the underlying's PD. On the other hand, PD information also exists in the option market, as we always need to consider for the option pricing the probability that the underlying reaches certain limits. Thus, with the help of cross-sectional pricing, we are able to connect the PD information of both credit and option markets as well as the strike of the American digital option, which is the only unknown parameter. We refer to this strike of the American digital option as the "strike of default" (SOD), which is the topic in our second and third paper. We obviously assume that the option market data and the CDS market data are available, since we deal with exchange-listed companies. Further, we assume that options and CDS contracts of the underlying are traded often, meaning the market data possess a certain level of credibility and liquidity. As we discuss later in more detail, there exists several CDS contracts with different maturities on the financial markets. Thus, we are able to derive a SOD value as long as option market data is available for the corresponding maturity. Without loss of generality, we presume that for the same company the value for the SOD decreases if the maturity of the SOD's increases. The reason for this presumption is that the price can drop in a longer period of time more before the company files for insolvency than for a shorter maturity.

In order to simplify the comparison between any two SOD values (either from the same company for different SOD maturities with the same evaluation date, or from the same company for different SOD evaluation dates with the same SOD maturity, or between companies on the same evaluation date with the same SOD maturity) we express the SOD in terms of "moneyness". In our case, moneyness is defined as the ration between strike and spot price. Because the strike is lower than the current spot price (otherwise the company is already defaulted due to our SOD hypothesis), the SOD value is a number between 0 and 1. It is obvious that the SOD cannot be negative, since the share price is always greater or equal to null. Hopefully we are then able to compare the risk profile of any two companies due to their different SOD's values. Further, we assume that without the consideration of the PD a company with a higher SOD is more likely to default, since the "risk buffer" (1—SOD) is smaller.

The SOD can be interpreted in two different ways. On the one hand, this SOD is a risk measure, meaning it gives a time-dependent benchmark measured in a share price. If such share price/benchmark is reached the underlying defaults. On the other hand, it can be viewed as a kind of hedging limit. For example, if a portfolio manager sells a CDS protection, the portfolio manager wants to know, if or when this protection is in any danger to be executed. To sell this CDS might be too expensive and then the SOD can guide the portfolio manager at which stock price preventions such as buying put option are necessary or even mandatory. In a best-case scenario, the portfolio manager executes the hedging interventions before the other market participants react. Further, the SOD is a risk measure and can help to understand a company's risk profile. Notwithstanding its interpretation, the SOD is purely based on market data and can change anytime between two trading days. Therefore, the SOD is a far more dynamic risk measure than the Kealhofer, Merton and Vasicek (KMV) model, where balance sheet data are needed. The KMV model is based on the structural approach. In the KMV model the default point is derived by the sum of short-term liabilities plus half the long-term liabilities, which again are very static parameters, whereas the SOD can be derived at any date. Without anticipation of any later results, we strongly believe that the concept of the SOD helps the monitoring and understanding of the default risk for companies which are listed on stock exchanges. Additionally we trust in the idea that the SOD can operate as an early warning system for anyone who bears a credit risk against an exchange-listed company.

The SOD is the main concept of this dissertation and all chapters and sections are lead to this concept. In this dissertation, we focus rather on the risk measure aspect than on the hedging aspect. We have added some minor findings concerning the hedging aspect of the SOD in the appendix. In the second paper, we go into detail on the derivation of the SOD and the calculation of the SOD. Especially the determination of the option price requires discussion in great detail. Then we determine the main parameters that influence the size of the SOD and construct a SOD function that is able to derive the SOD for maturities in between CDS grid points. Further, we analyse whether the SOD is influenced by the structure of the volatility surface and how the SOD between any companies behave. In the third paper, we study the sensitivity of the SOD input parameters and carry out a time series analysis with mainly two intentions: The first purpose is to examine whether the hypothesis of the SOD holds on our data set, i.e. that the company defaults once the SOD is hit during its particular runtime. The second purpose is to examine the influence of the company's SOD to its performance and whether the SOD is able to forecast the performance of the company to a certain degree. We complete the third paper by considering the theory of regulation by Stigler (1971) and the more general theory by Peltzman (1976) in the linear regression, regarding whether or not information that is government regulated is relevant for predictability purposes.

The structure of the dissertation
This dissertation is structured as follows. In Chap. 2, which represents the first paper of this quasi cumulative dissertation, we go into detail on the pricing methods of CDS contracts as mentioned earlier. We discuss several aspects on different ways to price a CDS contract such as different constructions for the survival respectively the default probabilities. Further, we explore different approaches on how to deal with time lags between the maturity of the index and its index-members. At last, we take a look at the influence of the use of different interest rate curves as discounting curves.

Chapter 3 is the main emphasis of this dissertation—the concept of our new developed risk measure or hedging limit which we call "strike of default" (SOD). In this chapter, which was accepted and presented at the World Finance Conference in Venice in July 2014, we derive in detail the idea and the range of applications of the SOD. In Sect. 3.3, we elaborate on option pricing methods in deep detail. The discussion about the four most important methods (namely Black-Scholes-Merton method, Monte-Carlo simulations, tree models and finite difference method) and their ability to price an American digital/binary option is the intention of this section. To the best of our knowledge, we derive a new method of pricing an American digital option with a binomial tree model. The discussion on the pricing of American digital options is very helpful and even necessary for the examining the deviation of the SOD. We then take a look at the derived SOD value for our data set and review our presumptions. Once we gain the SOD values for different SOD maturities, we are able to calculate the SOD function, which is spline interpolation to gather SOD values between the original grid points. Additionally, we examine the influence of the implied volatility surface's structure on the value of the SOD and compare the risk profile of any two companies based only on the SOD and with the consideration of the PD we gather from the CDS market quote.

In Chap. 4, which was accepted at the World Finance Conference in Singapore in December 2014, we investigate the sensitivity of the SOD according to its market input values. In other words we want to understand how the SOD changes, if the most important input parameters the CDS spreads and the implied volatility surface are shifted in either direction. Further, we test our SOD hypothesis that a company defaults once the SOD is hit in its duration based upon our data set. Finally, we set up linear regressions to observe the influence of the SOD on the underlying's performance. We use the SOD as the independent/variable of explanation and the performance as the dependent/explained variable. In an expansion of these linear regressions, we implement a regulation indicator for the purpose to consider the theory of economic regulation by Stigler (1971) and the more general theory by Peltzman (1976) stating that the "state protects the public" through regulation (in our case saving companies from bankruptcy).

Chapter 5, concludes the dissertation by reviewing the findings of each chapter as well as concluding the whole dissertation. Here, we also discuss several aspects that could be the topic of future research, especially in terms of the SOD.

We place some additional findings in the appendix of the dissertation that came along in researching these three papers. In Appendix A.1, we take a look at the behaviour of industrial sub-indices in the iTraxx Europe series 15 index, which was an additional outcome from Chap. 2. The companies, which are part of the iTraxx Europe series 15, can be categorised in five different industries such as the financial industry or the energy industry. We apply a linear regression to test whether these five industrial sub-indices, which are not equally weighted, have an influence on the index movement that differs from their actual weight of the index composition. For instance, our test aims to discover if the financial sub-index influences the index movements to a greater extent than the other sub-indices. In Appendix A.2, we derive an investment strategy using the SOD, i.e. applying the SOD as a kind of hedging measure. This investment strategy is purely based on the SOD information and the portfolios only consist of put options and CDS protection sells.

References

F. Black, M.S. Scholes, The pricing of options and corporate liabilities. J. Polit. Econ. (7), 637–654 (1973)

R.C. Merton, On the pricing of corporate debt: the risk structure of interest rates. J. Finance **29**(2), 449–479 (1974)

S. Peltzman, Toward a more general theory of regulation. J. Law Econ. 211–240 (1976)

G. Stigler, The theory of economic regulation. Bell J. Econ. Manage. Sci. 3–21 (1971)

Chapter 2
Different Approaches on CDS Valuation—An Empirical Study

Abstract In this chapter we want to discuss several approaches on the calculation of CDS prices. We apply different approaches in the hazard rate term structure, the influence of different interest rate curves used for discounting and the question of the price variation under the consideration of additional information will be discussed in detail. Further, we take a look how we can deal with constant maturity spreads in comparison to fixed maturity CDS Indices. Our benchmark is the iTraxx Europe index with different maturities of three, five, seven and ten years in comparison to its members.

Blythe Masters from J.P. Morgan & Co. invented the CDS in 1994. The market for CDS grew in the following years in a tremendous way. The volume invested in CDS products rose from about \$300 billion in 1998 to about \$62 trillion at the end of 2007. However, the CDS market is still an important sector in the financial markets. Even after the financial crises in 2007 and the following years, there was still 25 trillion dollars invested in CDS products. The influence of CDS investments was clearly demonstrated in April/May 2012, when JPMorgan Chase & Co., known as one of the top CDS trading banks worldwide, lost about two billion dollars within a few weeks as a result of speculative CDS trading.

In this chapter we take a look at different ways to price a CDS contract and the influence on CDS pricing by loosening some standard assumptions. There are basically two different approaches to evaluate a CDS contract. On the one hand, there is the structural form approach, and on the other, the reduced-form approach.

The structural form uses the option price theory on the company's value to gain the CDS spread. This approach is based on Merton (1974) and Black and Scholes (1973) and is the basis of the KMV model, which is used by some rating agencies. One key fact of this approach is that the probability of default is modelled indirectly. The problem of this model lies within the computation of the firm's volatility. Furthermore, this approach is rather inflexible, since it uses a lot of

---

This chapter is a working paper by Schmidt. See Schmidt (2014) "Different approaches on CDS valuation—an empirical study".

M. Schmidt, *Pricing and Liquidity of Complex and Structured Derivatives*, SpringerBriefs in Finance, DOI 10.1007/978-3-319-45970-7_2

information based on company actions and numbers that are only published on a few dates each year. In the scientific world, however, this approach is very popular and is used in many papers. There has been some interesting research on methods for improving this approach. Many papers use different kinds of volatilities such as implied volatility from out of the money puts see Cao et al. (2010) or Carr and Wu (2011). Other papers deal with the modelling of the recovery rate such as Li (2009). Even though this is a very interesting approach, we focus on the reduced form approach in this dissertation.

The reduced form approach is basically a method gathering the probability of default from an exogenous data such as ratings, bond prices or CDS spreads. Therefore, in contrast to the structured approach, the reduced form approach models the probability of default directly. The market standard model for the reduced form approach to CDS pricing is described by O'Kane and Turnbull (2003). Their description plays an important role in this dissertation. Pursuant to O'Kane's and Turnbull's assumptions, there are only a few parameters that determine the price of a CDS contract. These parameters are the recovery rate, the interest rate and the term structure of the so-called hazard rate. The hazard rate, or to be more precise the hazard rate term structure, is a method to model the probability of default or, respectively, the survival rate. O'Kane and Turnbull assume a partial constant hazard rate as well as a constant recovery rate. In the past, several research papers have been published on different approaches on a better method to model the recovery rate such as Li (2009), Krekel (2008), Amraoui and Hitier (2008) and Böttger et al. (2008).

In this chapter we discuss several approaches on the calculation of CDS prices and we test these approaches on historical market data quotes. For the empirical test we use a CDS index and we replicate the index by its constituencies. The CDS index we are using is the iTraxx Europe series 15 with different maturities of three, five, seven and ten years. Our ideas on the alternative pricing approaches are dealing with alternative hazard rate term structures, a multi-curve approach for the interest rates and the problem of maturity differences between the index and their member in the market data quotes. We describe each change later in detail.

This chapter comprises the following matters. In Sect. 2.1, we go into the details of the CDS single name and CDS index functionalities as well as the market standards by the International Swaps and Derivate Association (ISDA). For a better understanding we discuss several examples. In Sect. 2.2 we describe the standard method for CDS pricing using a reduced form approach. This chapter is based on O'Kane and Turnbull (2003). Section 2.3 explains how we are able to imply a hazard rate term structure and a probability of default (PD) from market data. Further, we explain the different hazard rate term structure that we apply in our research and how it is different to O'Kane and Turnbull (2003). The influence of the financial crises on the interest rates is specified in Sect. 2.4. We demonstrate the changes between different interest rate constructions and recapture the basic findings of Bianchetti (2010). Further, we explain the different interest rates in our approaches. Section 2.5 mentions the data set for our empirical test and the following Sect. 2.6 pictures our results. In the last Sect. 2.7 we draw a short conclusion on our results.

2.1 How Does a CDS Work?

In a CDS contract the investor, the so-called protection buyer, wants to secure himself against a credit event. This credit event can be attached to a company bond, a government bond or a basket existing of either or both. The protection seller guarantees the protection buyer to pay the outstanding loan in the case of a credit event. The outstanding loan is equal to the residual of the recovery rate times the nominal. The definition of a credit event can vary and needs to be clearly defined. In most cases a credit event is defined as bankruptcy or the failure to pay. In some case restructuring is also defined as a credit event. In return the protection seller receives a risk-adequate payment from the protection buyer. These cash flows are displayed Fig. 2.1.

The protection buyer can settle his obligation towards the protection seller with a single up-front payment at initiation, a regular coupon payment or a combination of both. The advantage of an up-front payment is that no future payments for the protection buyer exist. The size of up-front payment is equal to the present value of the regular coupon payments. However, the problem of the up-front payment is the uncertainty of the time of default. This problem cannot be explained in several notes. If you are more interested in this particular problem, please take a look at O'Kane and Sen (2003). The advantage of a regular payment is that it is a fair price, meaning no initial payment would be necessary, and the payments stop after a credit event. The disadvantage is the lack in tradability and comparison of CDS contracts on the same reference. Imagine two on-going CDS contracts on the same reference and the same maturity. The first contract has a regular payment of 230 bps

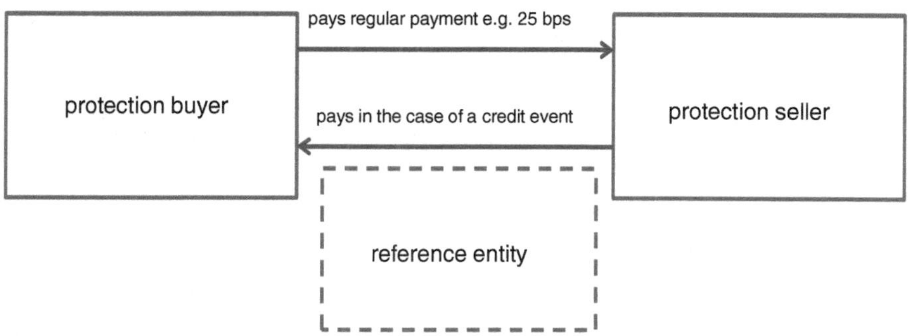

Fig. 2.1 In this figure, we observe the cash flows of a CDS contracts i.e. the regular payments of the protection buyer to the protection seller and the payment of the protection seller to the protection buyer in case of a credit event of the reference entity

and the second of 178 bps. Which one reflects the risk in a more accurate way? What if one of the parties would like to get rid of his position at the market? The advantage of a combination of both ideas is that the contracts are easy to trade, since the size of the regular payment does not change, and the changes in the market are dealt with a minor up-front payment. Minor up-front payment means that this up-front payment is not equal to the size of the single up-front payment as we discussed earlier. In fact, up-front payment does not necessarily have to be paid by the protection buyer, but more to that topic later on. For a detailed discussion about the differences between up-front and regular coupon payment take a look at O'Kane and Sen (2003).

The counterparties can agree on any of these payment schemes, which we just mentioned, since a CDS contract is an over-the-counter (OTC) derivative, meaning it can be tailor made. Due to the ambition of implementing market standards by the ISDA on the OTC markets, the most common way is to pay a regular coupon payment with an additional minor up-front payment. This regular coupon, which we refer to as contractual or deal spread, is denoted in basis points (bps). In case of a credit event the regular coupon payments stop, but the protection buyer has to pay the accrued interest (until the day of the credit event) to the protection seller. In Fig. 2.2, we monitor the cash flows in this particular payment agreement.

Example
Suppose investor "*A*" buys a CDS concerning company "*C*" from company "*B*" with a contractual spread of 100 bps and a nominal of €2,000,000. The payments are made in a quarterly frequency and the maturity is three years. We assume that in the case of a credit event company "*C*" has a recovery rate of 40 %. If there is no credit event until maturity, the investor "*A*" pays "*B*" about €5000 (≈2,000,000 * 0.01 * 3/12)—this amount can vary depending on the day count convention and the actual number of days—each quarter until maturity without any payments from "*B*" to "*A*". Let us assume a credit event occurs one week after a quarterly payment, then "*A*" would have to pay the accrued interest of about €385 (≈2,000,000 * 0.01 * 1/52).

Fig. 2.2 We see the payments made by both parties from the initial until a credit event. The arrows point towards the party that receives the payment. The first payment does not have to be done by the protection buyer sometime the protection seller needs to pay an initial up-front. The payment at default by the protection buyer is the accrued interest

Additionally, "*B*" has to pay the outstanding loan of €1,200,000 € [=2,000,000 * (1 − 0.4)] to investor "*A*".

Non tailor-made CDS deals use the market standards introduced by the International Swaps and Derivative Association (ISDA). These are standards in terms of coupon dates, day count convention, coupons per year, recovery rate, definition of a credit event etc. The coupons are paid on the 20th of March, June, September and December, which are the same dates as for futures and the dates are referred to as the IMM (International Monetary Market) dates. The date differences are calculated with the day count convention ACT/360, where the actual number of days between the dates is divided by 360. The recovery rate depends on the reference, but there are only a few values possible. For more information on the standardisation of CDS contracts take a look at markit.com.

It is very important to mention that we distinguish between the contractual spread and the market spread. The contractual spread is the size of the regular coupon and does not change for an existing contract until maturity. The market spread on the other hand, is the size of the contractual spread that the market believes to be fair for this particular underlying. In comparison to the contractual spread, the market spread change at any minute.

It is almost certain that at the opening of the CDS contract, a difference between market spread and contractual spread will be present. This difference can be priced and this price is what we called the up-front payment earlier. The relation between contractual and market spread with the addition of the accrued interest determines whether the protection seller or protection buyer needs to pay the up-front amount. Let us neglect the accrued interest for the moment. Three different states at the contract opening exist. First the deal spread is equal to the contractual spread. In this very unlikely situation no up-front payment needs to be done, because there is no difference between market and contractual spread. Secondly, the market spread is above the deal spread. This implies that the market believes the risk of the entity to be higher than the regular coupon. In this case the protection buyer has an advantage, since the protection is cheaper. Therefore, the protection buyer needs to pay the up-front, otherwise the protection seller does not agree on the transaction. In the last case, where the market spread is lower the contractual spread, the protection buyer receives the up-front payment, since the protection seller receives more than the market believes to be fair.

In general, the CDS price is notated in per cent just like bonds i.e. a clean price—which means without accrued interests—of 100 means that the contractual spread has the same size as the current market spread. The dirty price is the clean price plus the accrued interests. The up-front payment, from a protection buyer perspective, is then calculated via

$$\frac{100 - price_{dirty}}{100} * nominal$$

where a negative up-front means that the protection buyer receives the amount. The values for the protection seller are the same multiplied by minus one. Even though the standard price notation is in percentage you find the current market quote usually notated in basis points (bps) of the notional. There are some CDS securities that are not notated as a credit spread but instead as clean price. Examples are the CDX HY (Credit Default Swap index for high Yield Companies located in Northern America) and CDX EM (Credit Default Swap index for emerging market government bonds). Due to the ambition of market standards there are only a few contractual spreads used in the market (25, 50, 100 or 500 bps). The following example helps to gain a better understanding for the relations and notations.

Example
We would like to buy a three-year protection with a notional of ten million euros against a default of BASF on 2011-11-11. The current deal spread is 25 bps and the end of the day market quote is 78.3 bps. Then the clean price is about 98.57 and with an accrued interest of about 0.04 we derive a dirty price of 98.71. Then we would have to pay $(1 - 0.9871) * 10{,}000{,}000 = €129{,}000$ to enter this protection. Furthermore, we would have to pay each quarter about €6250 until the default of BASF or until 2014-12-20, whichever happens first.

In the case where a company holds a corporate bond and is secured by a CDS at the same time, the portfolio is not free of any risk. For example, the counterparty risk of the CDS protection seller still exists. For further information take a look at O'Kane and McAdie (2001).

It is possible to buy a CDS without holding a corresponding loan. This is called a naked CDS (sometimes called naked sell CDS or naked selling CDS). In this case the investor uses this position to speculate on the credit worthiness of the reference entity. There are estimations that assume the rate of naked sells to be about 80 % of the total CDS market. Also, it is discussed whether the naked sells support the negative trend of the credit worthiness of corporations or sovereigns. In this regard the Greek crisis is especially interesting. Since the credit spread rose in such an extreme way, which could be an effect from naked selling, the credit worthiness of Greece kept on sinking, also influencing the price of the government's bonds. That meant a cost increase to gather capital for the Greek sovereign on the financial markets. Consequently, the European Parliament has passed a ban on naked sells, where the reference entities are sovereign bonds, in the December of 2011. The EU believes that the dramatic situations as seen in Athens should not be repeated due to speculative investors' behaviour.

CDS indices
In recent years, CDS indices played a major role in the credit derivatives market. A CDS index consists of a number of CDS contracts that are clustered to a specific topic. In general, each index exists with different maturities (three, five, seven and ten years) and is rolled twice a year, meaning a newer version is placed in the market. The liquidity of these indices is always highest in the first six months and the first weeks after the roll (see Fig. 2.1). Within this new index the members can

be exchanged, the deal spread or the number of members can be modified, and so on. The indices can be divided into benchmark indices such as the iTraxx Europe and into topic indices like the CDX high yield (CDX HY). Unlike a single name CDS, which is determined after a credit event of the reference entity, the CDS indices exist further after the credit event of a member. In the case of a credit event in a CDS index, a payment in the default amount, which is equal to $(1 - R) * \frac{nominal}{number\ of\ members}$ and the nominal is reduced by $\frac{nominal}{number\ of\ members}$, will be made and the regular payment will be adjusted for the prospective payments since the face value decreased. The adjusted payments are expressed by a factor that represents the percentage of still existing members in the index. For example, if one member defaults and all other 124 members still exist, then this factor is equal to 0.992. The advantages of CDS indices are the simplification to hedge a portfolio of bonds against the possibility of defaults. Due to their standardisation, the indices are more liquid than single name CDS. Therefore, CDS indices often offer a smaller bid-ask spread leading to lower transaction costs than a single name CDS. Furthermore, the tradability and transparency for these CDS indices are higher than in a basket of cash bond indices or single name CDS.

There are two main CDS index families-the iTraxx and CDX family. In the CDX indices consist of CDS contracts on companies, which are located in North America, or of CDS contracts on sovereign bonds in emerging markets. As mentioned above, there are also some sub-indices like the high volatility index. The CDX indices are notated either in US dollars or in euros. The most common and liquid index within this family is the CDX investment grade (CDX IG), consisting of 125 North American companies with an investment grade rating. In the iTraxx family, CDS members are generally companies located in Asia or in Europe. The currencies within the iTraxx indices are the US dollar, the euro or Japanese yen. There also exist sub-indices like financial, Xover etc. Here, the most known and liquid index is the iTraxx Europe, whose 125 members are the most liquid companies in Europe during the last six months. In both index families a credit event is defined as either bankruptcy or the failure to pay. Additionally, in the iTraxx family a modified restructuring also counts as credit event.[1] The CDS indices play an important role within this chapter, since the index prices are the benchmarks for the different approaches we discuss later.

2.2 The Standard Approach for CDS Pricing

The standard approach for CDS pricing is described by O'Kane and Turnbull (2003). As mentioned above, this method is a reduced form approach. The CDS is divided into two separate legs. The premium leg represents the regular payments

[1]For further information on the CDX and iTraxx indices look at www.markit.com.

made by the protection buyer, and the protection leg simulates the payment by the protection seller in the case of a credit event.

The premium leg is priced like a bond with a fixed coupon. Additionally, we have to consider the probability of default as well as the necessary payment of accrued interest in the case of default. For reasons of simplification, for the pricing O'Kane and Turnbull assume that a credit event occurs always occur in the middle of two coupon dates. We can then derive the price of premium leg at time t as follows

$$\mathrm{premium}(t) = s_c \frac{1}{2} \sum_{n=1}^{N} \Delta(t_n, t_{n-1}) d_n (Q(t, t_{n-1}) - Q(t, t_n)) =: s_c * \mathrm{rcf}(t)$$

where N is the number of future coupons, t_n is the time in years between the n th coupon and t, d_n the discount factor from t to t_n, the parameter s_c represents the contractual spread and $\Delta(t_n, t_{n-1})$ is the time difference between the n th and the $(n-1)$ th coupon according to the agreed day count convention (ACT/360 as mentioned earlier). The function $Q(s,t)$ is the condition survival probability between s and t meaning the probability that there has not been a default until the time t given there was no default up till time s. Consequently we follow $Q(0,t) = SR(t)$, where SR is the survival probability. At this time we do not further discuss the form and derivation of $Q(s,t)$, but we come back to that topic later.

The pricing of the protection leg simulates the discounted cash flow in the case of a credit event. Even though it might take up to 72 calendar days between the notification of the credit event and the settlement of the protection payment, O'Kane and Turnbull assume that the protection payment is made immediately after the incident in order to simplify matters. For the validation of the protection leg, two factors are important, the recovery rate and the timing of the credit event. For the recovery rate, we assume that the historical recovery rate is the "correct" recovery rate. In our calculations, we always apply a recovery rate of 40 % because we only look at companies with an investment grade. Secondly, for the timing of the credit event we assume—without any material loss of accuracy—that the credit event only occurs on a finite number M of discrete points per year. Thus, we divide the maturity in a grid of $\lceil M * ttm \rceil$ discrete time points, where ttm is the time to maturity in years according to the day count convention. With a higher M we are able to gather more accurate validation of the protection leg, but the algorithm takes more time to evaluate. Therefore, like O'Kane and Turnbull we assume that $M = 12$, a simulation of a default once per month, is fine for our purpose. Then we gain at time t

$$protection(t) = (1 - R) \sum_{i=1}^{M*ttm} d_i (Q(t, t_{i-1}) - Q(t, t_i))$$

where R is the historical recovery rate, d_i is the discount factor between t and t_i and $Q(s,t)$ is same function as described above in the premium leg i.e. $Q(t,t_{i-1}) - Q(t,t_i)$ represents the probability of default within the ith coupon.

Under the assumption that we know the structure of the probability of default or the probability of survival respectively, we are able to gain the value of both legs. A transaction only takes place, if both legs have the same value. Thus, we can gain the adequate credit spread s for the deal at time t

$$s(t) = \frac{protection(t)}{\mathrm{rcf}(t)}.$$

As we see, the only input parameters varying depending on the respective company are the recovery rate and the probability of survival. Apart from the discussion about the correct risk free rate and the resulting discount factors, we are able to connect our opinion on a probability of default with a corresponding credit spread as seen in the market.

On the other hand, we are able to extract the corresponding probability of default from a market quote only using few assumptions. To imply the probability of default, we need to set the market quote equal to $s(t)$, since we defined the market quote as the contractual spread which the market believes to be fair. Then, we are able to price the CDS with this "implied" probability of default by setting $s(t)$ equal to the contractual spread, which we know in advance. In the following section we discuss the probability of default and the hazard rate term structures.

2.3 Probability of Default and Hazard Rate Structure

In the reduced form approach, a credit event is characterized as the first event of a Poisson counting process. That means we model the probability of a credit event in a time interval $[t, t+dt)$ under the condition that there has not been a default until time t as follows

$$P(\tau < t + dt \mid \tau \geq t) = \lambda(t)dt.$$

The function λ(t) is called the hazard rate term structure or just hazard rate. The equation leads us to the following model for the conditional survival probability until time T, if time t has been reached

$$Q(t,T) = \exp\left(-\int_t^T \lambda(s)ds\right).$$

Since we only want to evaluate the CDS at the trading date, meaning no forward CDS evaluation, this equation can be reduced to

$$SR(T) = Q(0,T) = \exp\left(-\int_0^T \lambda(s)ds\right).$$

This term is the same as the survival probability until time T, i.e. the condition dissolves, since we assume that the underlying has not defaulted before the pricing date. The following passages discuss several approaches on the construction of the hazard rate term structure λ(t). The survival probabilities always have to be arbitrage-free survival rates, i.e. then the CDS values in a risk-neutral world and the real world are the same. Therefore, the discounting factor is for our purpose the risk-free interest rate through the whole dissertation. Furthermore, the hazard rates are also arbitrage-free to fit the market values. Hazard rates based on historical data are higher, since they possess a liquidity risk premia, spread risk premia and so on.

2.3.1 Constant Hazard Rate

The first assumption is a constant hazard rate i.e.

$$\lambda \equiv \lambda(t) \text{ for all } t \in [0,T].$$

Due to this simple assumption the survival probability gets even simpler

$$SR(t) = \exp\left(-\int_0^t \lambda ds\right) = \exp(-\lambda t).$$

The parameter λ cannot be negative, because t is always positive and negative probabilities do not exist. Further λ cannot be zero, otherwise $SR(t) = 1$, meaning the probability of default $[P(t) = 1 - SR(t)]$ is zero.

The big advantage of this assumption is its simplicity and ability to gather fast results. In order to get the implied probability of default, we need to find a λ, so that the protection leg is equal to the premium leg, with the market quote being the contractual spread $s(t)$. A possible approximation to find λ is to guess an upper λ_{upper} and a lower λ_{lower} and then to apply a combination of the Newton and bisection method in order to derive the implied λ. The λ_{lower} can be close to zero, which means a high survival rate, and the λ_{upper} should be chosen high enough that $\lambda_{upper} > \lambda$. The approximation stops after a certain precision is reached. We are then able to price the CDS with the implied hazard rate and the contractual spread. The disadvantage of this method is, that it leads to different probabilities of default, if we look at different maturities.

Example
We collected the CDS spreads for BASF for maturities of one, three, five, seven and ten years on 2011-11-11. We then gathered the constant hazard rate like we

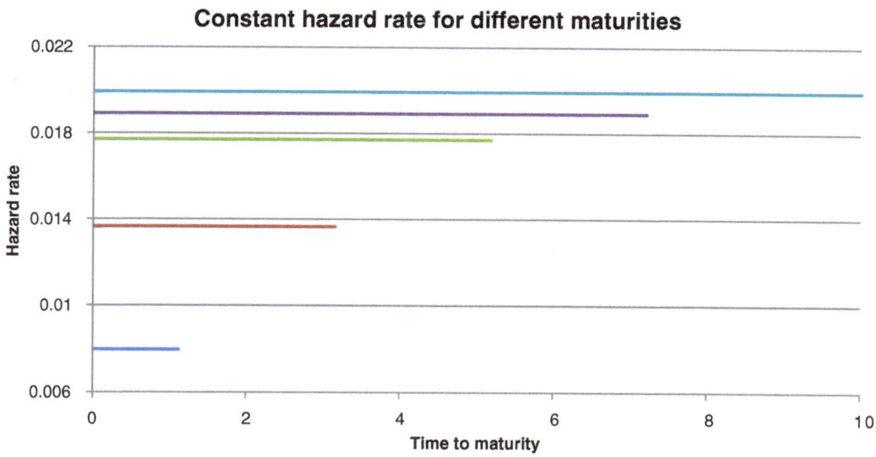

Fig. 2.3 The hazard rate under the assumption of a constant hazard rate term structure implied form the CDS market data for BASF on 2011-11-11

discussed above, see Fig. 2.3, and gained, as expected, higher constant hazard rates for longer life times. From this we can follow, that, depending on the hazard rate, we gather different probability of defaults for the same time period. For example, the probability of default within the first year, implied from the one-year CDS quote, is 0.79 %. Whereas the probability of default within the first year implied from to the three or ten year CDS quote is equal to 1.36 % respectively 1.907 %.[2] The corresponding curves showing the probability of default can be seen Fig. 2.4.

As we have seen in the example using a constant hazard rate can lead to different results for the implied probability of default. For each maturity, we gather different curves for the probability of default.

Why do we not use the additional information of different maturities to find a better approximation for the probability of default? We address with this idea in the next approach. Nevertheless, as we see later on, the constant hazard rate approach leads, on average, to a very good approximation for the index Value. Method and results are explained in more detail in Sect. 2.6.

2.3.2 Partial Constant Hazard Rate

In this approach we use all available market quotes from different maturities to bootstrap a unique hazard rate. All market quotes q_i are ordered according to their

[2]The results are based on the constant maturity quoted market spread for BASF CDS and on the interest curve, which was the standard interest curve before the crises. We refer to this interest curve as the single curve approach.

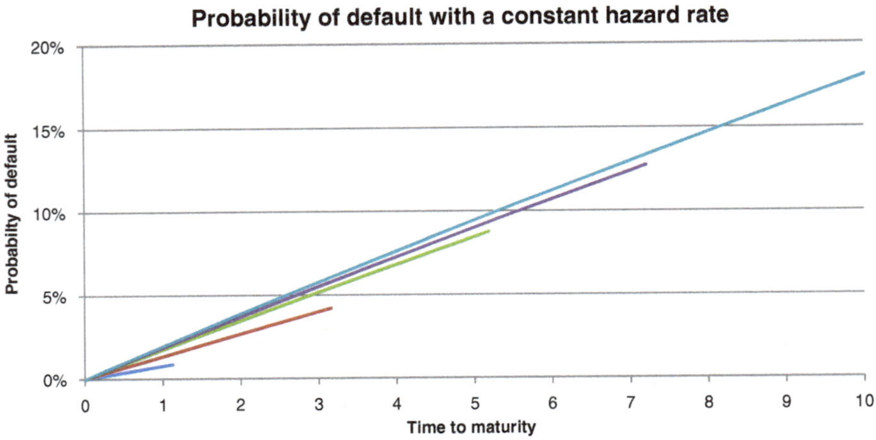

Fig. 2.4 The probability of default under the assumption of a constant hazard rate implied form the CDS market data for BASF on 2011-11-11

maturity t_i starting with the shortest t_1, which is the one-year maturity, to the longest maturity t_K of ten years, where K is the number of available market quotes. The hazard rate term is then built as follows[3]

$$\lambda(t) = \sum_{i=1}^{L} \lambda_i$$

with $L = min\{i | 1 \leq i \leq K \wedge t_i \geq t\}$. Consequently, the survival rate changes to

$$SR(t) = \exp\left(-t \sum_{i=1}^{L} \lambda_i\right).$$

The parameters λ_i are calculated from the market quotes q_i with the following bootstrapping algorithm. First, we determine λ_1 from the market quote q_1 in the same way as in the constant hazard rate case. Then, we extract the next parameter λ_2 and use for the survival rate

$$SR(t) = \exp(-t\lambda_1)$$

if $t \leq t_1$ and

$$SR(t) = \exp(-t(\lambda_1 + \lambda_2))$$

[3]This formula can also be written in the following form $\lambda(t) = \sum_{i=1}^{K} \lambda_i 1_{\{t_i \geq t\}}$, where $1_{\{t_i \geq t\}} = 1$ iff $t_i \geq t$ and else zero.

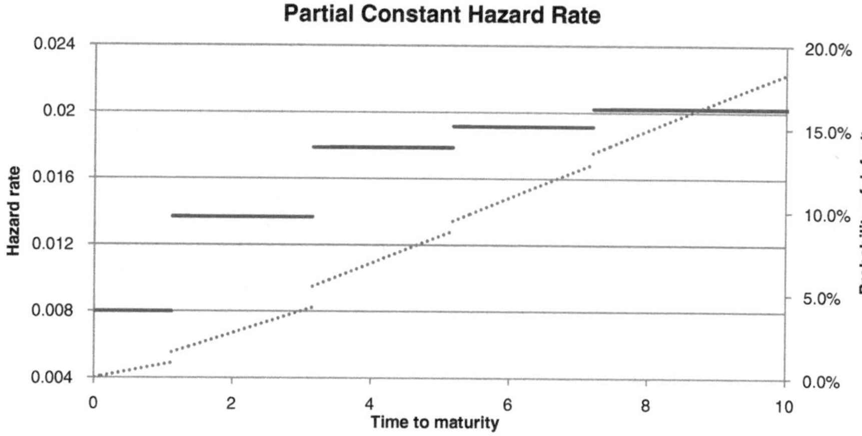

Fig. 2.5 The hazard term structure (*blue straight line*) and the probability of default (*red dotted line*) under the assumption of a partial constant hazard rate implied from the CDS market data for BASF on 2011-11-11

if $t_1 < t \leq t_2$. Like in the constant hazard rate approach, we use a combination of the Newton and the bisection methods to calculate λ_2. For all following maturities, we apply the same strategy as described for the second maturity, until we reach the last maturity K.

Example
We consider the same case as before, i.e. BASF CDSs on 2011-11.11. This time we gain that the probability of default within the first year is 0.79 %. Also, this time only one hazard rate exists. Therefore the corresponding probability of default is unique. The corresponding data is shown in Fig. 2.5.

The advantage of this approach is that all market data are implied and there is only one probability of default curve. Nevertheless, some disadvantages exist. Firstly, the method takes longer computing time to gain results for longer maturities. Secondly, more market data are needed. Thirdly, the quality of the data can be different between maturities, but this disadvantage affects all approaches. At last, it is very likely that the probability of default curve is discontinuous and jumps at each maturity of a market quote.

2.3.3 *Linear Hazard Rate*

The simplest idea to gain a more realistic and smoother probability of default curve is to use a linear hazard rate. Like in the constant hazard rate case we first take a look at the different CDS maturities on their own, meaning we gain one hazard rate for each maturity. Subsequently the hazard rate term structure is modelled via

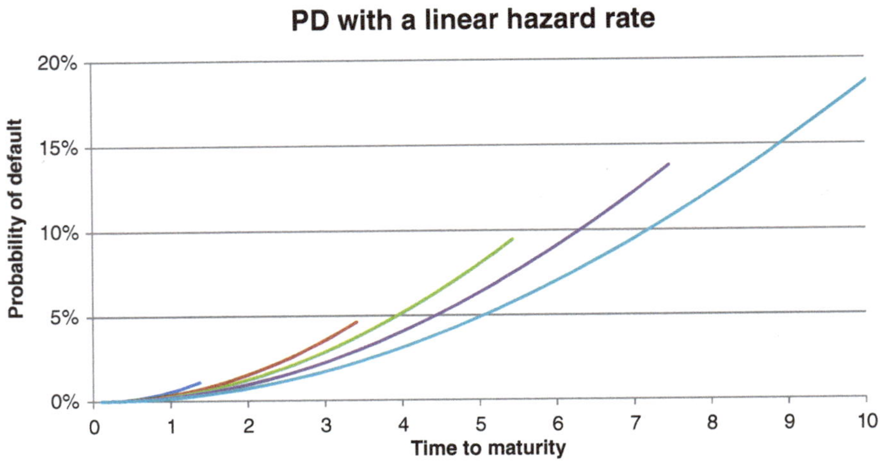

Fig. 2.6 The probability of default under the assumption of a linear hazard rate implied from the CDS market data for BASF on 2011-11-11

$$\lambda(t) = \lambda t$$

and the corresponding survival rate is given by

$$SR(t) = \exp\left(-0.5\lambda t^2\right).$$

The deviation of the parameters λ_i is the same as described in the constant hazard rate but this time with a survival rate modelled like the equation above.

Example
In our standard example this leads us to different hazard rates as well as different probabilities of default. For example, we gain for the probability of default within the first year based on the one-year CDS a value of 0.71 %, based on the three year CDS quote a value of 0.44 % and based on the ten year CDS quote a value of 0.21 %. At first, it is surprising that the probability is decreasing for longer maturities whereas in the constant hazard rate case the probability of default is increasing for longer maturities. This is due to the fact, that in the linear hazard rate case the probability of default curve is not linear but quadratic and therefore the probabilities for longer maturity are more "weighted" than shorter maturities (see Fig. 2.6).

2.3.4 *Partial Linear Hazard Rate*

Lastly, we want to use a partial linear hazard that combines the linear approach as well as the idea of using all available information from all market quoted CDS

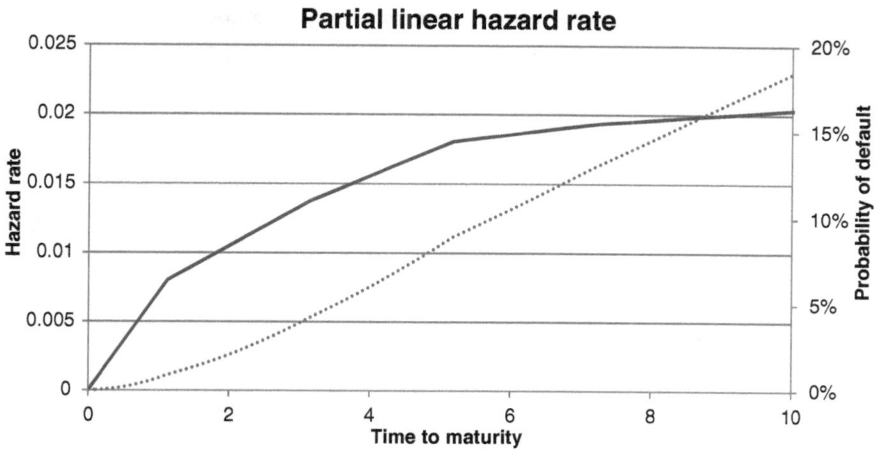

Fig. 2.7 The hazard rate term structure with a partial linear hazard rate (*blue straight line*) and its corresponding probability of default (*red dotted line*) implied form the CDS market data for BASF on 2011-11-11

spreads.[4] We use the same method as before. First, we gather the hazard rate λ_1 following the linear hazard rate case. Then, we drive λ_2 and so on until we reach λ_K. In this model we assume that the hazard is constructed in the following way

$$\lambda(t) = \sum_{i=1}^{L} \lambda_i t$$

with $L = min\{i|1 \leq i \leq K \wedge t_i \geq t\}$ and the corresponding survival rate changes to

$$SR(t) = \exp\left(-0.5t^2 \sum_{i=1}^{L} \lambda_i\right).$$

Thus, in this model the hazard rate is never the same at two different time points, and if we assume $\lambda_i > 0$ the hazard rate is a monotone increasing function.

Example

If we consider our standard example again, we gain a probability of default of 0.71 % for the first year which, as mentioned above, is the same as in the linear case. The results of this example are plotted in Fig. 2.7.

As we can see from this example, the partial linear smoothly combines many advantages and only one probability of default curve exists. Nevertheless, there are

---

[4]A similar approach has been demonstrated by O'Kane and Turnbull (2003).

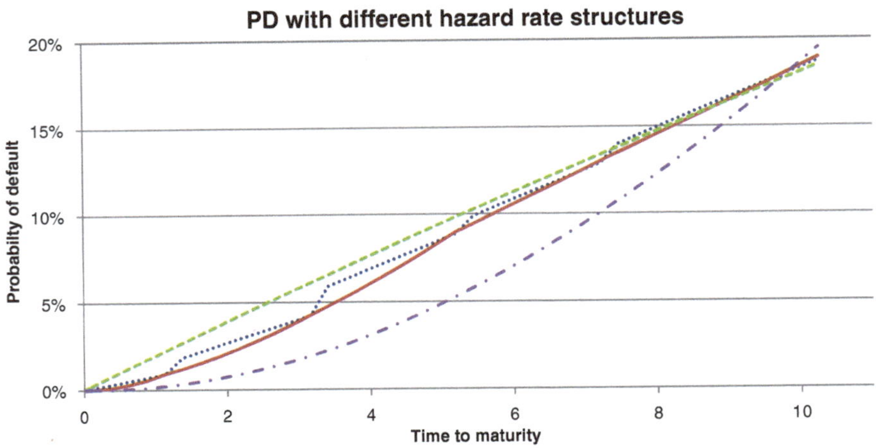

Fig. 2.8 The probability of default with different hazard rate structures, where the *red straight line* stands for the partial linear approach, the *blue dotted line* for the partial constant method, the *green disrupted line* for the constant (for the ten-year contract) and the *purple, dashed line with dots* represents the linear methods (again for the ten-year contract) implied from the CDS market data for BASF on 2011-11-11

also some disadvantages. In the linear case, for example, we find the property that $P(t<s|t\geq r)=\exp(-\lambda(s-r))$ i.e. the probability of default in a given time $(r-s)$ always stays the same. This does not apply in any of the other models.

Of course, it is possible to apply other hazard rate structure terms such as a quadratic polynomial and higher. However, the results show that a higher degree does not lead to a more precise pricing.

In the following Fig. 2.8 we combined all different models. Again, we see that the partial linear case is the combination of the linear and the partial constant approach. We discuss the advantages and disadvantages later along with the results.

2.4 Multi Curve Approach

In this chapter, we briefly discuss the differences in the yield curves before and after the financial crises. As an effect of the financial crises of 2007, the need for a multi curve approach grew. In other words, using a single interest rate curve for discounting as well as for forward rate calculation regardless the tenor was not adequate anymore. This was due to the fact that the basis spread quoted on the market had increased tremendously as demonstrated in Fig. 2.9. The plot shows the difference in prices between a basis swap for a three months EURIBOR against a six months EURIBOR basis swap, both with a maturity of five years. We see the price difference was negligible until the 3rd quarter of 2007. However, with the

Fig. 2.9 This graph pictures the historical price differences between the three months EURIBOR basis swap with a maturity of five years against the six months EURIBOR basis swap with a five year maturity

beginning of the credit crunch, its value began increasing and has not stopped since, i.e. it shows the increase in liquidity between these two tenors.

This effect can also been observed if we take a look at basis swaps with different tenors and maturities as displayed in Fig. 2.10. We recognise that the basis swaps spread is the highest for short term contracts as well as for contracts of which the

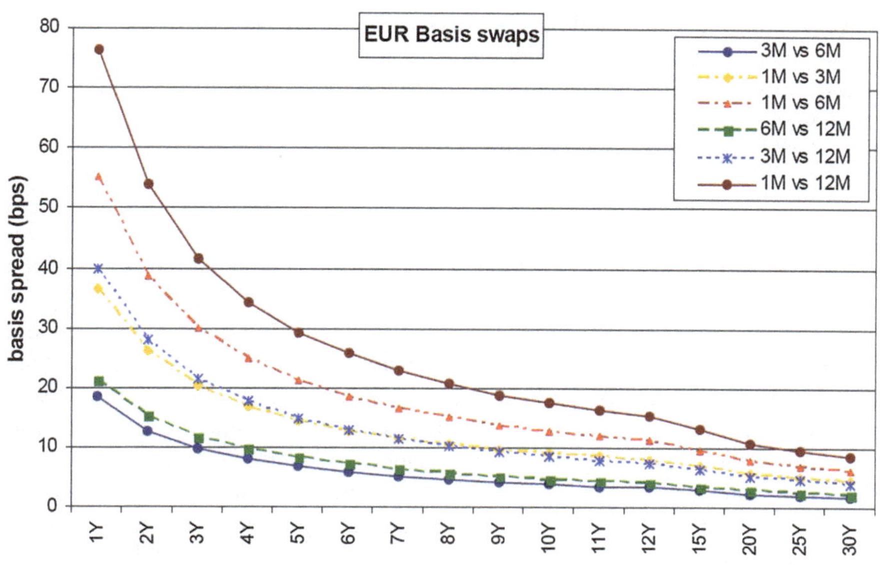

Fig. 2.10 This figure from Bianchetti (2010) demonstrates the difference in the swap rates due to their tenor and maturity

tenors are further apart (time wise) from another. The spreads vary from nearly 80 bps for a one-month versus twelve months (1 M vs. 12 M) basis swap contract with a maturity of one year to about 2 bps for three months against six months (3 M vs. 6 M) basis swap contract with a maturity of thirty years.

All these observable effects are due to a higher counterparty risk as well as a higher liquidity risk after the credit crunch of 2007.

Pre-crises Market Practice for yield curve construction

The standard market practice before the credit crunch was based on a single curve approach. In other words, only one valid yield curve was used for discounting as well as for forward rates calculations. The procedure is to gain one unique yield curve from the most liquid interest rate products via a bootstrapping method. For example, in the Eurozone it was very convenient for the short term to use the EURO deposits, i.e. the EURIBOR spot rates with a maturity up to one year, for the medium term FRAs/futures/swaps on the three months EURIBOR and for the long term, maturities longer than two years, swaps on the six months EURIBOR. Then the forward rates r_f in time t for the time interval $[t_1, t_2]$ could be calculated via

$$r_f(t; t_1, t_2) = \frac{B_z(t, t_1) - B_z(t, t_2)}{\tau_x(t_1, t_2)\, B_z(t, t_1)}$$

where $B_z(t, t_1)$ is the price for a zero bond at time t expiring in time t_1 and $\tau_x(t_1, t_2)$ being the year fraction between t_1 and t_2 using the day count convention x.

Post-crises Market Practice for yield curve construction

The above approach is no longer valid, since it fails to take several effects into consideration. First, the single curve approach does not take the basis swaps into account, which are no longer negligible as seen in Fig. 2.9. Secondly, the approach does not consider the segmentation of the interest rate market into sub-areas that correspond with different instruments with distinct underlying tenors such as one, three, six or twelve months. We still assume the arbitrage free discounting must be unique.

The procedure to gain multiple curves is first to gather a unique discounting curve $\mathrm{r_d}$, which for example can be the same as the curve we gain from the single curve approach. Bianchetti (2010) writes about the construction of the discounting curve as follows "we stress that the key first point in the procedure is much more a matter of art than of science, because there is not a unique financially sound recipe for selecting the bootstrapping instruments and rules". Subsequently, we need to build distinct forwarding curves $\mathrm{r_{f_i}}$ for different tenors i, which typically are one, three, six or twelve months. The bootstrapping can be done for each forward curve by using the interest rate products with the same tenor (as the desired forward rate curve) and under the consideration of the unique discounting curve. Finally the basis swap spreads between the different curves can be calculated as follows

$$BS_{id}(t, t_1, t_2) = \frac{B_{z_d}(t, t_2)}{B_{z_i}(t, t_2)} \frac{B_{z_i}(t, t_1) - B_{z_i}(t, t_2)}{B_{z_d}(t, t_1) - B_{z_d}(t, t_2)}$$

where BS_{id} is the multiplicative basis swap spread between the curve with tenor i and the discounting curve. We gather the additive basis swap spread very easily via

$$BS'_{id}(t, t_1, t_2) = r_{f_d}(t, t_1, t_2) \left[BS_{id}(t, t_1, t_2) - 1\right]$$

with r_{f_d} as the forward rate using the discounting curve. It is obvious, that in the single curve approach $BS_{id}(t, t_1, t_2) = 1$ and $BS'_{id}(t, t_1, t_2) = 0$.

Because the multi curve approach strongly depends on the discounting curve, several practices for the construction of the discounting curve exist in the market. According to Bianchetti (2010), there are mainly two different methods in the market. On the one hand, some market participants use the "pre-crisis" curve for discount i.e. spot, FRA/futures (three months tenor) and swap (six months tenor) basis, which we refer to as the "single curve". On the other hand, other participants apply the OIS (overnight index swap) curve, which we consider to be the best approximation for a risk free counterpart. In Fig. 2.11 we see the differences between these two curves. With this figure we can first support the "pre-crises" thesis, meaning there was no need for a multiple curve approach. If you compare the top lines in Fig. 2.11, we see that they are nearly the same, i.e. no basis swap spread. Secondly, we can encourage the tremendous effect of the basis swap spread after the crises and the need for an adequate discussion about the proper discount

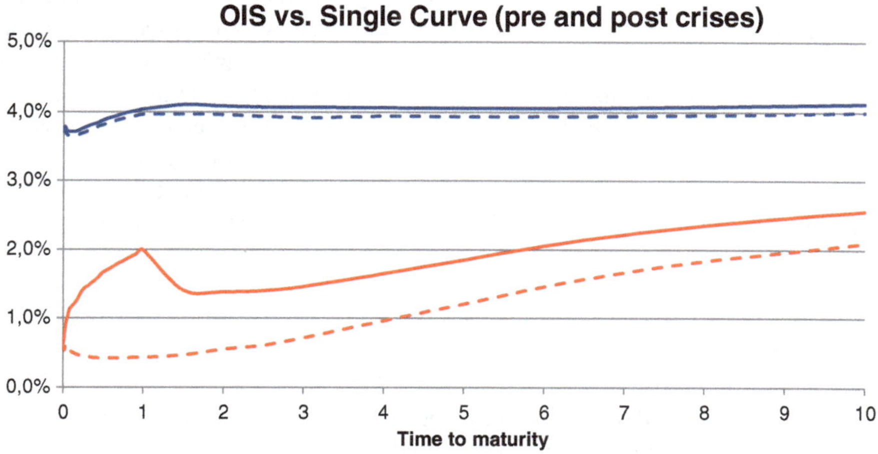

Fig. 2.11 These are examples of interest rate term structures before and after the financial crises with the OIS and the single curve approach, where the pre-crises curves are *blue* ones with the OIS method curve being interrupted and the after crisis are *red* with the OIS method curve again being interrupted

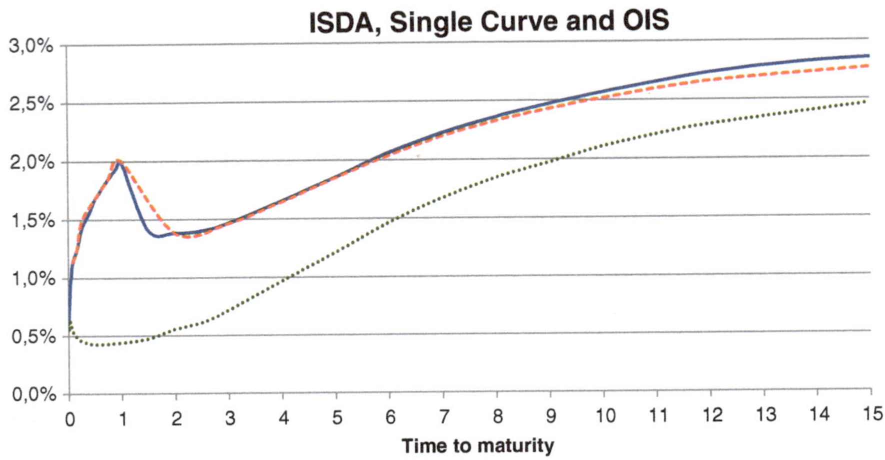

Fig. 2.12 We plotted the different interest rate structures on the 2011-12-21, where the *blue line* is the SC approach, the *red interrupted line* the ISDA curve and the *green dotted* the OIS approach

(or risk-free) yield curve. Furthermore, it is worth noting that the curves after the crises are not monotonic increasing functions anymore.

In this dissertation, we take a look at the influence of different discounting curves on the CDS evaluation. Most CDS deals are based on the ISDA convention with their "own" ISDA interest rate, which is published every day. This curve is based—at least for the euro discounting curve—on the spot rates of the EURIBOR up to one year and on the swap rates for maturities longer than one year. This is similar to the single curve and as we observe in Fig. 2.12, these yield curves are almost the same. Their differences are probably caused by different time points, since the ISDA curve is based on the 11.00 o'clock Frankfurt values for the spot rates and the 16.00 o'clock Frankfurt values for the swap rates and our single curve is based on end of day data from Frankfurt. The OIS curve represents the rate that can be seen as the most *risk-less*[5] curve. Therefore, the OIS curve can be seen as the curve in which the counterpart is a central counterpart. If we compare the derived prices using the same hazard rate structure but different interest rate curves for discounting, we can interpret these differences as the price for the counterparty risk.

2.5 Data Set

We collected end of day CDS quotes from all members or constituencies of the iTraxx Europe series 15 with maturities of one, three, five, seven and ten years. That means we collected end of day quotes from up to 625 securities per day from

[5]Due to the experience of the financial crisis we circumvent the term risk-free.

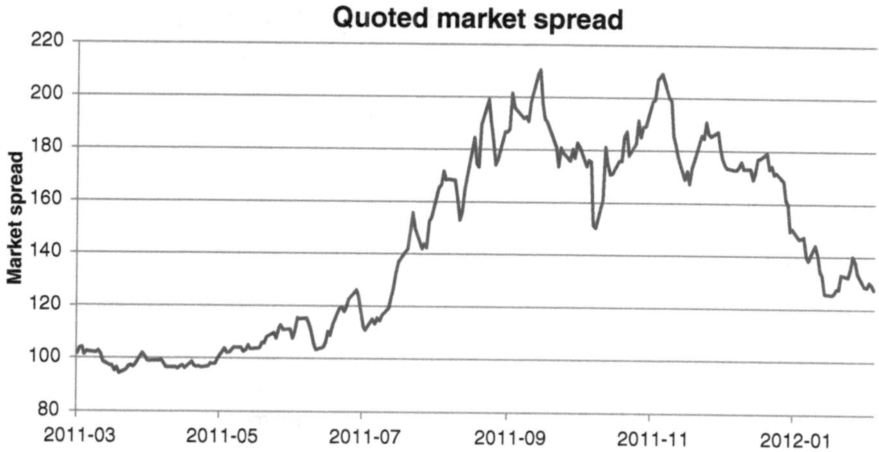

Fig. 2.13 This graph shows quoted market spreads for the five year iTraxx Europe series 15 with a contractual spread of 100 bps

Thomsen Reuters via Datastream. We gathered the end of day quotes for the iTraxx Europe series 15 indices itself from Markit. Our first day of observation is 2011-03-21 and the last is 2012-02-24, the development of five-year iTraxx Europe series 15 can be seen in Fig. 2.13. On 2011-03-21 the iTraxx indices were set up, meaning we collected nearly the whole first year of all CDS quotes for the indices and their constituencies. End of day quotes means the last traded quote on that particular trading day and thus the timestamps are not identical for all quotes. Until the iTraxx Europe series 16 started on 2011-09-20, the iTraxx Europe Series 15 was the current iTraxx index or as it is called the "on the run" index. It has been mentioned in several papers that the CDS market is the most liquid for contracts with a maturity of five years. In Fig. 2.14 we show the money invested in the 5-year iTraxx Europe series 15 to support the statement that the indices are the most liquid while they are "on the run".

It is important to mention, that a slight problem concerning the maturity of the CDS deal exists. The maturity date of the indices obviously keeps the same until it is reached, e.g. 2014-06-20 for the indices with a runtime of three years starting on 2011-03-021. The maturity date for the index members always differ, since there is a roll every quarter. In other words, the CDS contracts for the constituencies never reach their maturity date. This phenomenon is also known as constant maturity contracts. For example, let us assume the CDS of a member such as Kraft Food with a runtime of five years. Then its maturity date is 2016-06-20 of the CDS quote during the dates 2011-03-20 and 2011-06-19. However, the maturity date changes to 2016-09-20 for the quotes from 2011-06-20 to 2011-09-19 due to the roll on 2011-06-20. Therefore, only in the first quarter of the index all the CDS quotes from the members have the same maturity as the index. In our case, that is from 2011-03-21 to 2011-06-19. Thus, we have to find a way to build an adequate

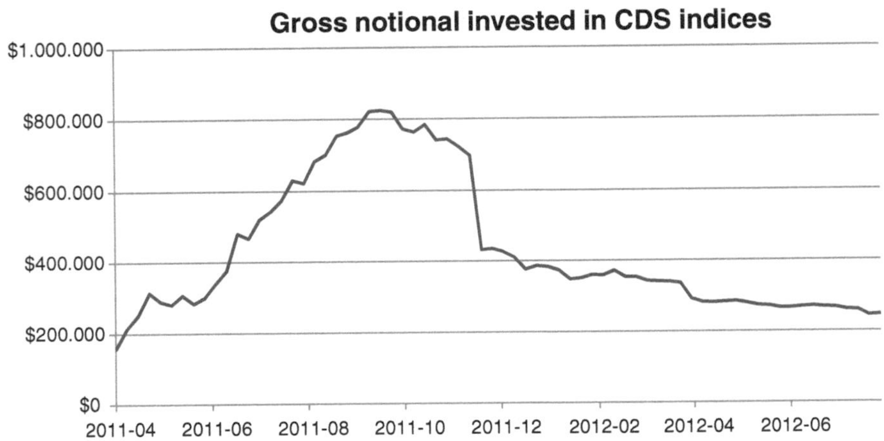

Fig. 2.14 We display the gross notional amount invested in the CDS indices measured in million USD for the iTraxx Europe series 15

market quote for the constituencies for the time interval 2011-06-20 to 2012-02-24. Therefore, we always need a shorter maturity of the index member to be able to interpolate between market quotes. That is the reason why the one-year quote is necessary for each member, even though there is no iTraxx index with one-year maturity.

As noted above, the question of the proper CDS quote rises. For example, what is the proper quote for a contract with a maturity of four years and nine months, if we only have a quote for a maturity of five years and three months and a quote for a maturity of three years and three months? There are several ways to deal with this problem and we try three different approaches to handle it. First, we use the constant maturity quotes to price the CDS even if the maturity of the index and the maturities of the index members differ. Secondly, we apply the constant maturity quote again, but this time we only extract the hazard rate structure from its original maturity and apply it to the maturity of the index. For example, let us assume a constant hazard rate on the three-year index with its maturity on 2014-06-20. On 2011-11-11 the maturity of the constant three-year CDS quote is on 2014-12-20. According to this market data approach we imply a constant hazard rate of the members calculated with their correct maturity (2013-12-20), but we price the CDS by applying the hazard rate to the maturity of the index (2014-06-20). We refer to this market data approach as "the constant maturity applying to the index maturity". Ultimately, it is possible to interpolate in between the two closest runtimes e.g. using the five and three year constant maturity CDS contract to imply the market quote for a maturity of four years. An interpolation can have different degrees for the polynomial, but for reasons of simplicity, we apply a linear interpolation. Further research could investigate the difference of higher-degree interpolation.

2.6 Results

We calculate the CDS prices for the indices as well as for the members in several ways. We use two different interest rate curves, single curve and OIS as mentioned above. We utilise the following different hazard rate structures: constant, partial constant, linear and partial linear, as described earlier in Sect. 2.3. Since we have an additional problem with the proper market data for the CDS of the index member, we use yet another three different approaches. The market data approaches are (i) the original constant maturity, (ii) constant maturity applying to the index maturity and (iii) the linear interpolation between two constant maturities spreads with different maturities. To sum up, we calculate CDS prices with eight different methods for all indices (two interest rate and four hazard rate structures) and CDS prices with 24 different methods for all members (additionally three methods for the market data). Then we determined the average of all CDS members to gain an index replication. As an alternative index replication we apply the members' median. Since this approach leads to values that are of much greater value in comparison to the average, we do not want to discuss this approach in detail. That means, we calculated the replication as follows

$$R_{index}(t, ir, hr, md) = \frac{1}{125}\sum_{n=1}^{125} CDS_n(t, ir, hr, md),$$

where t is the date, ir the used interest rate, hr the hazard rate structure and md the market data. Then we derived for each day

$$\hat{R}_{index}(t, ir, hr, md) = (Index(t) - R_{index}(t, ir, hr, md))^2$$

and for the whole time of observation

$$\tilde{R}_{index}(ir, hr, md) = \frac{1}{N}\sum_{t=1}^{N} \hat{R}_{index}(t, ir, hr, md).$$

Before we go into detail on the replications results, let us analyse the impacts of the various hazard rates structures as well as the differentiation between the interest rate curves on the price of the CDS indices.

First, let's take a look at the difference hazard rate structures, i.e. the relations between index prices determined with different hazard rate structures. With a larger maturity, the absolute differences to the prices rise between the different structures, this finding is not surprising. Obviously this is due to the fact that up to three years the methods are not so different or even the same as in the constant and the partial constant or as in the linear and the partial linear case. Further, the longer the maturities are, the more noticeable the differences in the approaches become. If we consider our example of BASF on 2011-11-11 again and compare the constant and

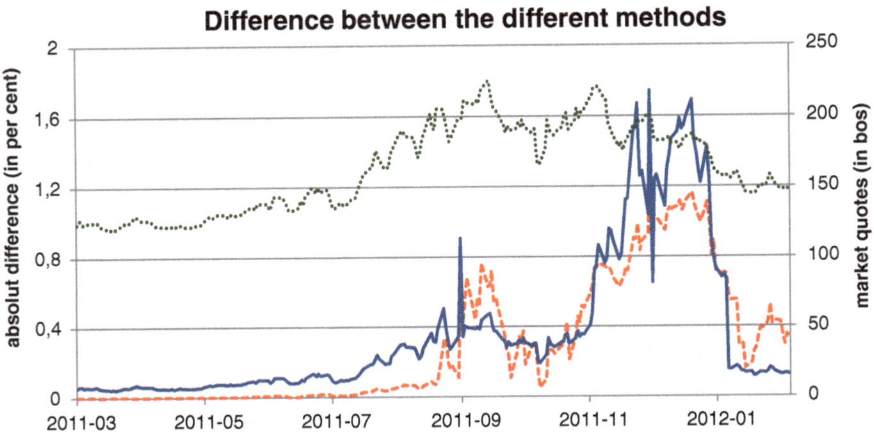

Fig. 2.15 This figure shows the absolute difference between the index calculated with different hazard rates, where the ten year iTraxx Europe difference is represented by the *blue line*, the five year iTraxx Europe difference is displayed by the *red interrupted line* and the *green dotted line* is the market quote of the ten year iTraxx Europe. Note that the CDS prices are denoted in percent. Therefore, this difference is an absolute value and not a relative one

the partial constant hazard rate structure for a ten-year contract, we notice that in case of the constant hazard rate, the probability of default (PD) is about 1.907 % in the first year. But in the partial constant approach the PD over the same time horizon is only 0.79 %. These results show that early payments are weighted more heavily in the constant hazard rate structure. Therefore, their prices are (slightly) higher than in the partial constant approach. Further, in the partial constant hazard rate approach, in the first year, the PD is extracted from the one-year CDS quote and not from the ten-year CDS quote. The following two graphs support this statement. In such graphs, we display the (maximum) absolute difference between the indices prices of the five and ten year contract.

The differences in the iTraxx prices are rather large (up to 1.76 %) as shown in Fig. 2.15. From all hazard rate structures (constant, partial constant, linear, partial linear) we observe, that the constant hazard approach most often (in about 76 % of all results) leads to the highest calculated price, whereas the linear case mostly bears the lowest price (about 62 %). For maturities greater than five years the price always (!) is the highest if we assume a constant hazard rate and if the lowest price for these maturities is calculated either with a linear hazard rate (86 % of all dates) or with a partial linear hazard rate (14 %, or the rest of the dates). This shows that if we only use a single market quote, which is the case for the constant or the linear hazard rate structure, we subsequently gain a greater difference in calculated CDS prices, i.e. the choice of hazard rate term structure becomes more crucial.

In the next step, we examine the different interest rate curve for the iTraxx contracts. First, we draw the attention to the differences within the interest curves. There are two main facts in the behaviour of the curves. First, they differ the most in

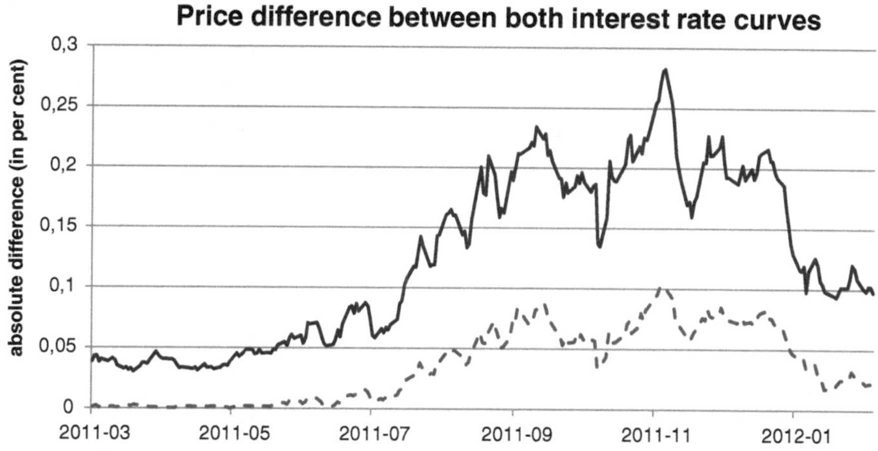

Fig. 2.16 This figure plots the absolute difference between the calculations with both interest curves, where the *blue line* represents the difference for the ten-year maturity and the *red interrupted line* for the five-year maturity

the first few months as we observe in Fig. 2.12. Secondly, the curves converge to each another the longer their runtime. We assume the prices to differ more for the shorter maturities, since the curves are varying the most. Therefore, it is surprising that the difference between the index prices with the single curve and the OIS curve is increasing with maturity. Nevertheless, the prices' difference between the interest rate curves, under the assumption of the same hazard rate structure, only leads to an absolute value of 0.31 % (i.e. 31 bps). With maturities greater than five years, the OIS approach always delivers a lower price than the single curve approach. Figure 2.16 demonstrates the absolute difference between the prices for five and ten year maturities and also shows the increase of the price differences during longer maturities.

If we loosen the assumption that we compare the price difference for different interest curves with the same hazard rate structure, i.e. we compare all eight prices with each other, the price range grows (up to 1.97 i.e. or nearly two percent) and with longer maturities the OIS approach always delivers a lower price than the single curve approach does.

The choice of interest rate curve also affects the implied PD of the referenced underlying if we assume the same CDS spread. As we can see in Fig. 2.17, where we calculated the difference in the implied PD until maturity under the assumption of a linear hazard rate, the PD is always higher under the single curve assumption. Since we can argue that the OIS curve is more likely to be "the interest rate with the lowest risk involved", we can interpret this PD difference as the counterparty risk or, more precisely, the risk that the reference entity as well as the counterpart does default simultaneously. This topic can be widely discussed but it is not the matter for discussion in this dissertation.

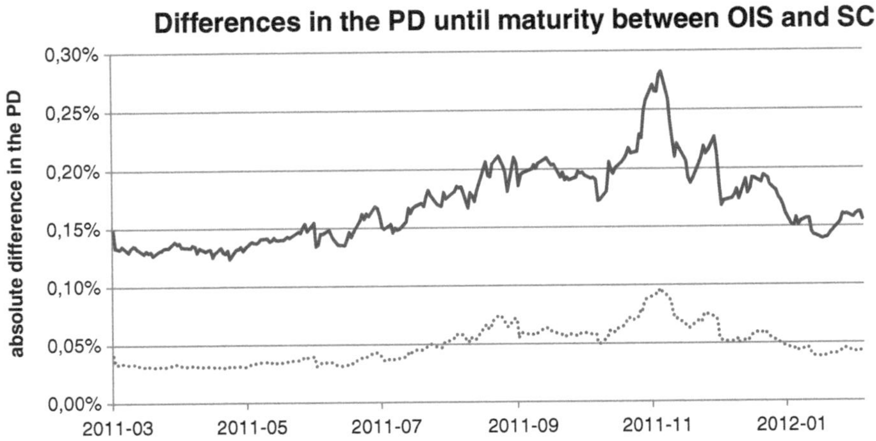

Fig. 2.17 This figure displays the difference in PD until maturity between a determination with the OIS or with the single curve approach, where the *blue line* stands for the ten-year maturity and the *red interrupted* for the five-year contract

Lastly, we analyse the different approaches combined with the topic the proper market quote for the index members according to the price differences between the index and the mean of the index member prices. Before we go into the results in detail, it is worth mentioning that all methods lead to more or less acceptable prices. Nevertheless, some methods lead to an absolute percentage difference of about 2.6 %, i.e. index price being about 90.36 and the replication being about 92.72. As seen before, that means it is not negligible which assumption we consider if we want to derive a CDS price. The following results are all based on the comparison between the index results and the results of replication. The replication values differ more the longer the maturities of the contracts are. The difference $\hat{R}$ ranges from 8 bps on average over all approaches for the three-year contract to 69 bps on average for the ten-year contract. Concerning the optimal market data we would assume, that the constant maturity approach is the worst, since it does not fit the maturity of the index, followed by the interpolated market quote, due to the inaccuracy of the market quotes. We would also assume that the implied hazard rate from the constant maturity quotes applied to the index maturity will lead to the most precise result. However, this presumption only fits either for maturities no longer than three years or if we exclude the linear hazard rate approach from our result set. This is not an absurd conclusion, because the results of the linear hazard rates distort the overall results. The results reveal that the longer the maturity, the better interpolated market quotes, followed by the constant maturity market quotes and finally the implied hazard rate applied to the index maturity. We can observe such results in Table 2.1, where we calculated the $\tilde{R}$ for all different approaches including crossings. With "crossings", we mean different approaches for the evaluation of the index and index members.

Table 2.1 Here the average values in bps for different maturities are shown. Obviously represent smaller values a better approximation to the pricing index. Each value is based on 242 points of observation

Market data (in bps)	3 Years (n = 242)	5 Years (n = 242)	7 Years (n = 242)	10 Years (n = 242)
Total average	7.90	16.81	37.11	68.91
Const. maturity	14.20	16.80	30.85	66.96
Implied to index mat.	3.99	19.37	47.31	74.33
Interpolated Quotes	5.51	14.28	33.18	65.44

Further, we compare the deviation if the indices and the members are subject to the same hazard rate structure ignoring the market data quote for the members. The data reveal that the approximation with a linear hazard rate structure is without any doubt the worst as we see in Table 2.2. For maturities up to five years the constant hazard rate structure seems to be the optimal choice, for longer maturities the additional market information—the "partial" approaches—deliver more precise results.

At last, we look at different hazard rates structures for the indices and the members, e.g. the constant hazard rate is applied for the index but the members are evaluated with a partial linear hazard rate structure. The results are mapped in Table 2.3.

If we focus on hazard rate structure for the members, we imply that the hazard rate structures being more complex always provide a lower $\tilde{R}$ and therefore a better approximation to the index than the approach, which is simpler. For the approximation of the index, this means it is better to apply all CDS data information available. In our case, this means the "partial" methods dominate the "non-partial" methods. For example, with a partial constant hazard rate structure for the index, the partial linear approximation is better for the members than the linear approximation (28.31–36.51). For the various index hazard rate structures, the effect is not as dominant as before. There still exist cases where a "partial" method dominates the "non-partial" method. For example, if we apply the partial linear hazard rate

Table 2.2 Here, the average values in bps for different hazard rate term structures are shown. Smaller values obviously represent a better approximation to the pricing index. Each value is based on 242 points of observation

Hazard rate index (in bps)	3 Years (n = 242)	5 Years (n = 242)	7 Years (n = 242)	10 Years (n = 242)
Total average	7.90	16.21	35.92	65.95
Constant	5.74	12.87	32.51	67.67
Linear	9.74	21.99	49.75	79.20
Partial constant	8.43	14.04	28.42	60.55
Partial linear	7.70	15.96	32.99	56.38

Table 2.3 The different hazard rate structures for the index and the members are shown with their average difference over all maturities and the maximum difference during our observation period. Obviously smaller values represent a better approximation to the pricing index

Index hazard rate	Members hazard rate	$\tilde{R}$ (n = 888)	Max. value
Constant	Constant	29.70	184.71
Constant	Linear	36.49	184.84
Constant	Partial constant	28.45	187.95
Constant	Partial linear	28.94	184.31
Linear	Constant	36.51	204.73
Linear	Linear	40.17	209.36
Linear	Partial constant	31.71	193.55
Linear	Partial linear	31.51	189.91
Partial constant	Constant	29.63	186.71
Partial constant	Linear	36.51	186.85
Partial constant	Partial constant	27.86	189.96
Partial constant	Partial linear	28.31	186.32
Partial linear	Constant	40.69	214.66
Partial linear	Linear	39.00	244.47
Partial linear	Partial constant	29.22	191.13
Partial linear	Partial linear	28.26	187.48

structures for the members, then the index replication is more precise for the index price evaluated with a partial constant hazard rate structure (28.31) than for the index price evaluated with a constant index hazard rate (28.94). There also exist some counter examples such as the constant hazard rate for the members and the constant respectively partial constant hazard rate structure for the indices. Nevertheless, all different combinations have about the same magnitude of possible maximum differences per day. In other words, the choice of the hazard rate structure for the CDS valuation does not protect for higher difference during the replication of a CDS index. These differences between replication and index can still be caused by their difference in liquidity or simply by the quality of the data.

2.7 Conclusion

The choice of the hazard rate structure can lead to different CDS prices. The consideration of further CDS market data can lead to better approximations and a more realistic mapping of the probability of default. On the one hand, these approaches need more valuation time and market data. The problem of market data with different maturity is that the quality and the liquidity can differ, which always remain a doubt to the calculated results. On the other hand, the results show that the valuation with a constant hazard rate structure—based on a single CDS market quote—is a solid implication for quick information.

According to our research, for CDS contracts with a different maturity than the available constant maturity contracts, the best approximation is the linear interpolation between available CDS market data quotes. If we do not assume a linear hazard rate structure, it is even better to use the implied hazard rate from a market quote with a longer maturity to evaluate the CDS contract. For the index with a runtime of three years, the best approximation is to use the constant three-year maturity CDS market quote for the constituencies.

The selection and determination of an interest rate curve can be important especially for longer maturities. The interest rate curve also determines the probability of default and the counter party risk, which shall be of special interest in the combination of a central counterpart.

We observe that CDS pricing valuation is not as straightforward as one might assume. Each approach has its legitimation and there is no single "correct" way to price a CDS. All impacts are more important and more noticeable for longer maturities. The results show, that the longer the maturity, the more complex is the valuation—complex in the sense of hazard rates (partial constant or even partial linear) as well as market data. Having said this, an even more complex approach such as cubic spline interpolation and a quadratic hazard rate structure could be an interesting topic for future research as well as a the usage of recovery models.

References

S. Amaraoui, S. Hitier, Optimal stochastic recovery for base correlation. BNP Paribas (2008)

M. Bianchetti, Two curves, one price: pricing & hedging interest rate derivatives decoupling forwarding and discounting yield curves. Risk Mag. **10**(8), 70–75 (2010)

F. Black, M.S. Scholes, The pricing of options and corporate liabilities. J. Polit. Econ. (7), 637–654 (1973)

M. Böttger, A. Guthoff, T. Heidorn, Loss given default—Modelle zur schätzung recovery rates. Working paper (2008)

C. Cao, F. Yu, Z. Zhong, The information content of option-implied volatility for credit default swap valuation. J. Finan. Markets **13**(3), 321–343 (2010)

P. Carr, L. Wu, Stock options and credit default swaps: a joint framework for valuation and estimation. J. Finan. Econometrics **8**(4), 409–449 (2010)

M. Krekel, Pricing distressed CDOs with base correlation and stochastic recovery. Working paper (2008)

H. Li, On models of stochastic recovery rate for base correlation. MPRA (2009)

R.C. Merton, On the pricing of corporate debt: the risk structure of interest rates. J. Finance **29**(2), 449–479 (1974)

D. O'Kane, R. McAdie, Trading the basis. Risk Mag. (2001)

D. O'Kane, S. Sen, Up-front credit default swaps. Lehman Brothers fixed income quantitative credit research (2003)

D. O'Kane, S. Turnbull, Valuation of credit default swaps. Lehman Brothers quantitative credit research quarterly (2003)

M.F. Schmidt, Different approaches on CDS valuation—an empirical study. Unpublished working paper (2014)

Chapter 3
Credit Default Swaps from an Equity Option View

Abstract We compare the implied probability of default on the credit market and on the equity market of the same underlying. In order to compare these two different markets, we use the price of premium leg of a CDS contract as the price for an American digital option. If called, this option pays the same amount as the protection seller (CDS) in a credit event. The applied volatility will be extracted from implied volatility surface. Via an optimization procedure we find the corresponding strike to the option price which we call "strike of default". This number can be seen as a risk measure or an individual hedging limit for this underlying hence the markets assume a default at this share price with the maturity of the CDS.

In this chapter, we take a different look at the valuation respectively the perspective on CDS products. The idea is to compare the default risk implied in the CDS market with the default risk implied in the option market. In other words, we combine CDS spreads with traded options with the same underlying. From the protection seller point of view, a CDS contract tends to be like an American binary option since the pay-off is fixed, if we assume a constant and pre-trade known recovery rate, and since the credit event can occur at any time until maturity, the option has to be provided with an American exercise style. Furthermore, we assume that the option is exercised as soon as it is in-the-money, i.e. if the strike K is reached, and therefore, according to both markets, the underlying defaults. This last assumption is straightforward, because the option payoff does not depend on the moneyness, which is the ration between stock price and strike. Further, this assumption is a special case of Carr and Wu (2011), where the bottom of the so-called default corridor is equal to zero. For the valuation of the options we apply volatilities, which we extract from the implied volatilities surface, for deep out-of-the money (DOOM) American put options. We use the implied volatility surface, because several studies have shown that implied volatilities are a better fit than historical volatilities such as Cao et al. (2010). These American binary options are of course

This chapter is a working paper by Schmidt. This paper was accepted and presented at the World Finance Conference in Venice in July 2014. See Schmidt (2014)—"Credit Default Swaps from an equity point of view".

M. Schmidt, *Pricing and Liquidity of Complex and Structured Derivatives*, SpringerBriefs in Finance, DOI 10.1007/978-3-319-45970-7_3

synthetic as they rarely exist on the market—probably only in the OTC-market—or, if they exist, only with a low liquidity. Concerning the options pay-off, we model it in a way that the protection seller, who we assume buys these options, is perfectly hedged against the credit event of the reference. This means the options pay-off has the same volume as payment of the CDS protection seller in case of a credit event. The payment amount of a credit event is equal to $(1 - R) * Nominal$, where R is the recovery rate of the underlying. The maturity date of the CDS contracts and the American binary options are constructed to be the same. We evaluate the CDS contracts as well as the option data on the base of end-of-day (EOD) quotes/prices, i.e. we assume that the spot price of the share and the spot quote of the CDS contract are roughly from the same time point. Further, the CDS quotes are mid quotes, i.e. the average between bid and ask quote. The only remaining parameter for the option pricing is the actual strike. We assume that the strike depends on the maturity as well as on the underlying's implied probabilities of defaults from both markets.

Our aim is to find the corresponding option strike for the CDS, i.e. at what asset price—before or at the maturity of the CDS—the market believes that the entity will default. We presume that this "strike of default" (SOD) depends on the maturity, the size of the CDS quote as well as the volatility surface and its structure. Thus, the SOD is a synthetic benchmark of cross-sectional pricing. Furthermore, we use the available grid points to derive an SOD function to gain the SOD for different maturities. In an optimal case, we are able to compare the default risk of any companies based on their SOD. This is an improvement to the CDS data, because the SOD also contains the data from the option market. In Fig. 3.1 we show the basic idea of the SOD with a possible stock price. We demonstrate two possible stock price developments with two different strikes for different maturities.

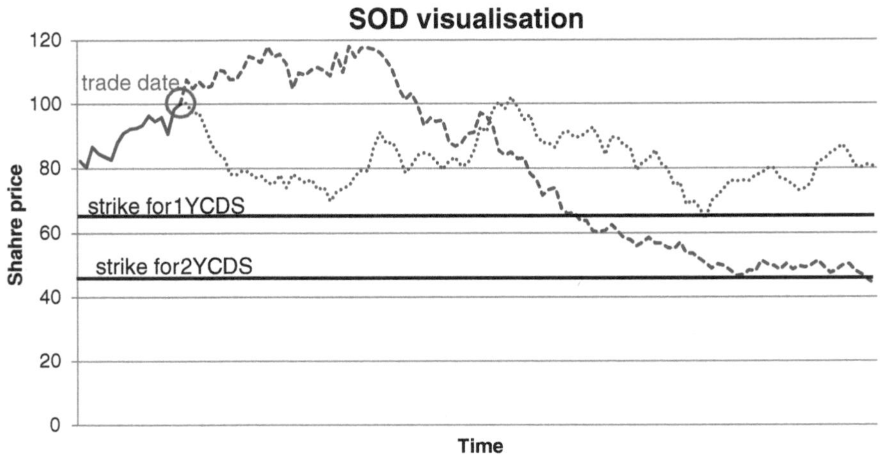

Fig. 3.1 This graph plots two simulations of the same share price with two possible strikes of defaults for different maturities

The SOD translates the probability of default (PD)—from the credit and the option market—into a time depending threshold denoted as a share price. This threshold can be seen as a risk measure on the particular underlying. Further, the SOD can be used as a hedging-limit for the CDS protection seller, meaning if the asset price moves closer to the SOD the protection seller needs to be prepared against a much more likely default of the underlying. Apart from Carr and Wu (2011) who extracted a default corridor, which is an interval of stock prices, our approach is the first to link the PD to a single stock price.

There are already several papers published which recognised the linkage between implied volatilities of options and the credit default spread on the same reference entity such as Collin-Dufresne et al. (2001) or Zhang et al. (2009). Hull et al. (2004) proved, with their new implementation and estimation method for the structural model of Merton (1974), that the changes in at-the-money volatilities and in the CDS spreads are locally perfectly correlated. The research of Byström (2005) support that statement and he also found out that the CDS spreads are negatively correlated to the stock price. Carr and Wu (2009) showed a framework between stock options and credit default swaps. They conclude that deep out-of-the-money (DOOM) American put options prices are mainly driven by the probability of default and are more sensitive the longer the maturity of the option is. Cao et al. (2010) proved that implied volatilities are more suitable to forecast the credit spread than historical volatilities.

Some publications also address CDS valuation with option implied volatilities such as Cao et al. (2010), wherein the authors use a modification of the structural approach to price a CDS. Their finding is that implied volatilities are more robust than historical ones. Carr and Wu (2011) developed a robust link between DOOM American put options and so-called unit recovery claims (URC). A URC is a contract, where the protection buyer receives one dollar if and only if the reference entity defaults before or at maturity. They introduced a default corridor $[A, B]$, where the stock price an never reside within this corridor, meaning the stock price is either above the barrier B or, if it falls below B, a default is automatically triggered and the stock price jumps underneath the barrier of A. Further, they proved that if this corridor exists, a vertical spread of stock American put options scaled by the difference in strikes has the same payoff as a URC. Based on Carr and Wu (2011) paper Angelopoulos et al. (2012) revealed that large cross-market deviations in option prices and in CDS spread of the same entity enclose valid information on the future stock price.

This chapter continues as follows. In Sect. 3.1 we introduce the idea of the SOD in more detail with a special focus on the assumption of the input data. The next two Sects. 3.2 and 3.3—deal with the determination of the CDS price as well as the evaluation of the American digital option. Section 3.4 describes the data set and the results are described in Sect. 3.5. In Sect. 3.6 we draw the conclusion of this chapter.

3.1 Introduction to the SOD

The aim of a CDS is to guarantee a payment in case of a default of the reference underlying,[1] meaning the payment of the protection is unknown—we can even say the payment is "optional". The size of the payment at default is known, if we assume the recovery as familiar. Therefore, the payment of the protection seller can be seen as a binary option. Since the default event and especially its time point are unknown, the execution of the binary option has to follow the American exercise style. We interpret payments made by the protection buyer as the premium of this option. The premium of the CDS is equal to the sum of the discounted future coupon payments, which are also weighted by the probability of default. Further, we assume that the share price and the market CDS spread are negatively correlated. That means, if the share price increases, the CDS spread will decrease and vice versa. Therefore, we are able to find an equity option that fits the CDS premium, but there are still some unknown parameters as we see later on. Byström (2005) proved a negative correlation between CDS spreads and the stock prices. As an example of the negative correlation between CDS spread and their corresponding stock price, we compare the stock price of Deutsche Bank with their five year CDS in Fig. 3.2.

For the pricing of any option, we need the following information: The underlying spot price, time to maturity (ttm), the strike, the volatility, the exercise style (American, European, Asian etc.), direction (put/call) and a pre-defined pay-out schedule. In general, we also need dividends, but since we look at the SOD, we easily assume that the price of the underlying share decreases over time and the entity therefore is not able to distribute any dividends. The pay out schedule is $(1 - R) * \mathit{Nominal}$ with R the recovery rate, if the option is exercised, otherwise there is no payment. The direction of the option has to be a put since there will only be a credit event, if the share price drops—vice versa the credit spread rises—and the execution style must be American, as discussed earlier. The spot price of the underlying option is the current equity price at the moment of the transaction or CDS quote. We apply end-of-date quotes and prices for our approach. As mentioned earlier, we use volatilities, which we extract from implied volatilities surfaces depending on the ttm and the strike. Unfortunately, we generally cannot apply implied volatilities, because the strike is too low for the implied volatility surface. The exact procedure will be discussed later on in a separate section, for now it is enough to know that a proper volatility is available. The only remaining question is the size of the proper strike, meaning the determination of the strike K is the real task. We assume that the strike for CDS with a maturity of one year is higher than the strike of a CDS with ten-year maturity, because the opposite does not make any sense. Imagine the share price of any company would cut in half within a year or within ten years. Then we assume the first case to be more dangerous to the further

[1]It is worth mentioning at this point that the case of bankruptcy always counts as default whereas restructuring usually is not defined as a default.

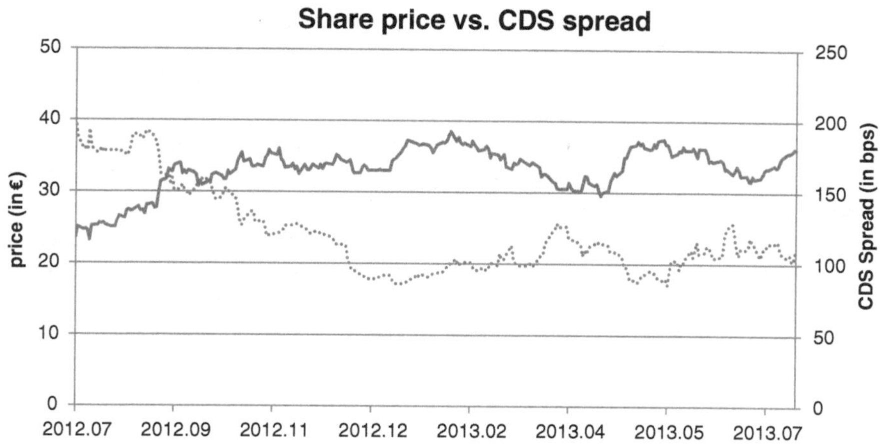

Fig. 3.2 This figure displays the share price (*straight line*) against the five-year CDS spread (*dotted line*) of the Deutsche Bank. The correlation during that time series between the share price and the CDS quote is −0.83

of the existence of the company than the latter case. If we interpret the SOD as the time-depending stock price at which the underlying does default, a higher SOD for a longer maturity does imply that the underlying defaults more easily on the long term than on shorter terms. Therefore, we assume a decreasing SOD with increasing maturities, i.e. a monotonic decreasing function.

For the protection seller, the size of the SOD is important, because the strike delivers a hedging level as well as a benchmark when the protection seller gets worried that the protection payment will have to be paid with a reasonable probability. As mentioned earlier, we derive the price of this binary American option via the price of the CDS premium leg, meaning we have to match the option price to the price of premium leg via the fitting of the strike. Because we use a volatility that depends on the moneyness and therefore on the strike, we apply a different volatility once we change the strike.

3.2 CDS Premium Fee

The standard pricing methods for a CDS contract are described in detail in Sect. 2.2. The deviation of the PD and, respectively, the hazard rate structure are explained in Sect. 2.3. For deviation of the SOD we apply a constant hazard rate term structure as well as the single curve approach as described in Sect. 2.4. Further, we always use the constant maturity CDS, because there is no need to fit a CDS contract to an index. In fact it is quite the opposite: We construct the option to fit the CDS' maturity.

For our purposes, in a first step we derive the implied hazard rate from the market quote. In the next step we only calculate the premium leg, where we apply the deal spread and extracted hazard rate. We only use the premium leg, because we interpret this leg as the value of the option fee. In the market, a protection buyer also needs to pay the accrued interest. One can argue that for our synthetic propose the accrued interest is not of any interest, but on the other hand, if you buy a default protection through a CDS contract, the accrued interest always needs to be paid. Therefore, we observe both prices: one price considering premium leg plus accrued interest, called the dirty CDS-option price, and one price considering the premium leg only, disregarding the accrued interest. We will refer to the latter price as the clean CDS-option price.

3.3 Option Pricing

The strike of default (SOD) is a risk measure that is derived from CDS and option market data. We discuss the deviation of the SOD in Sect. 3.1 in detail, but we need some preparations first in order to calculate the SOD. In order to fully understand the concept of the SOD we need to be familiar with CDS and option pricing. The CDS pricing was the main topic of Chap. 2 and was repeated for our use in Sect. 3.2. Thus, we address the topic of option pricing. It is a brief overview of the major option pricing methods used in practice. Not all methods can be applied to every option type since there are many different types of options. For example, some options are path-dependent which can lead to a complicated pricing method and sometimes the Monte-Carlo simulation remains as the only practical method. Nevertheless, for some options close-form solutions exist, whereas other options need the stock price history for the deviation of the options pay-off.

In an option contract the owner has the right, not the obligation, to buy (call) or sell (put) a certain underlying asset to a determined price (strike) at maturity (European exercise style) or up until maturity (American exercise style). This definition describes what is known as a plain vanilla option. The underlying asset can vary from shares, currencies, commodities and many more. For the rest of this dissertation, we always look at options on exchange-listed companies. For example, we assume that the current stock price is at €100 and we buy an option that allows us to buy the share at a price of €110 in one year's time. Or, to put it in shorter words, we buy a call with a spot price at €100, the strike at €110 and with a maturity of one year. Then, we only exercise this option, if the share price is above €110 in one year—otherwise the option is worthless.

As mentioned above, a lot of different variations of options exist in the market. For example, there are options, where the share price needs to reach a certain level for the options to get activated or deactivated. In other options, the pay-off depends on the movement of the share in a certain time frame and so on. For the deviation of the SOD, we need to evaluate American digital/binary (put) options. These are options where the payoff is fixed in advance, i.e. the payoff is known at contract opening. This is the reason why they are called digital or binary—only to possible outcomes exist, either an exercise with fixed payment or no exercise at all. Further, these options can be exercised at any time until maturity, i.e. the American exercise style. Since this option does not depend on the share price, we assume that the option is exercised as soon as the strike price is reached without any loss of generality. At last, we construct the American binary options in a way that the payoff is equal to the payment of a CDS in case of a credit event, meaning in case the strike is reached the option's pay-off is equal to $(1 - R) *$ nominal with R being the recovery rate and nominal being the amount invested in the CDS contract.

Mainly, four different methods for option pricing currently exist. These are the Black-Scholes formulas or more general closed-form solutions, the Monte-Carlo simulation, the tree models (binomial and trinomial) and the finite differences (implicit, explicit and Crank-Nicolson). Before pricing an option one needs to ask oneself, which pricing method can be used to this particular option type and which is the best to use. For our brief overview, we assume that the asset S follows the simple stochastic process

$$dS = \theta(r - \mu)Sdt + \sigma\theta SdW_t,$$

where r is the risk-free rate, θ is the speed of the process, μ the mean of the asset, σ^2 the volatility of the asset and dW_t is the Wiener process or standard Brownian motion. If we only take a look at the first part on the right side of the equation, we observe that the process is deterministic and the asset price reaches its mean μ depending on its speed θ. This type of process is called mean reverting due to the fact that process always return to its mean μ. The latter part on the right hand side joins a stochastic part. The Wiener process is a continuous stochastic process with independent normally distributed increment meaning $W_t - W_s \sim \mathcal{N}(0, t - s)$. This stochastic process also is a Markov-process, which means that the future states of the asset only depend on the current state and not on historical prices. Like in the CDS evaluation, we apply that there are no arbitrage possibilities and the discount factors are based on the risk-free interest rate. Therefore, the option price in the real world and in the risk-neutral world must be equal.

Many expansions of this stochastic process exist. Most of these variations deal with the applied volatility, since it is the biggest unknown parameter in the stochastic process. Here we only mention Heston (1993), due to its significant influence. In the Heston model, the volatility follows a stochastic process, an Ornstein-Uhlenbeck process, which we are able to convert with the Itô lemma into a square root process also known as CIR (Cox et al. 1985), to be precise, itself. For the determination of option prices, we use implied volatilities or respectively volatilities, which are interpolated on an implied volatility surface.

In the following sections, we discuss each option pricing method in general and how this approach helps us with the SOD deviation. Without anticipating too much we need to be able to price an American binary option for the SOD deviation. Furthermore, the option price will be given and we need to be able to determine the corresponding strike. For a deeper and more detail understanding of the approaches, take a look at the book *Options, futures and other derivatives* by Hull (2012) or at *Paul Wilmott on quantitative finance* by Wilmott (2013).

3.3.1 Black-Scholes-Merton

The Black-Scholes formulas, based on Black and Scholes (1973) and Merton (1974),[2] are closed-form solutions for options with a European exercise style. These formulas are part of the closed-form solutions, which are generally speaking theoretical option prices, which can be derived with some straightforward formulas. The Black-Scholes-Merton formulas are probably the most known formula in financial mathematic. Furthermore, these formulas had a tremendous impact on the success and development of financial engineering in the 1980s and 1990s. In 1997 Robert Merton and Myron Scholes received a Nobel Prize in economics their research. Unfortunately, Fischer Black had already passed away in 1995 and could therefore not be included in the awarding of the prize. It is always very comfortable to find a compact form or even a single formula to be able to calculate the desired outcome.

The main basic assumptions for the Black-Scholes formulas are, (i) a random walk for the log return of the asset, (ii) a constant risk-free interest rate exists, (iii) there are no arbitrage opportunities, (iv) lending and borrowing any amount at the risk-free interest rate is possible, (v) there are no transaction costs and (vi) selling and buying any amount of asset is also guaranteed. In the original approach, the underling stock was assumed not to pay any dividends, but the formulas were further developed in a way that this assumption is no longer necessary. The deviation of the Black-Scholes formulas is rather long and thus we only repeat the formulas for European options. Then the option prices of a stock option is theoretical given by

$$c = Se^{-qT}\Phi(\mathrm{d}_1) - Ke^{-rT}\Phi(\mathrm{d}_2)$$

and

$$p = Ke^{-rT}\Phi(-\mathrm{d}_2) - Se^{-qT}\Phi(-\mathrm{d}_1),$$

where c is the price for a call option, p is the price for a put option, K is the strike of the put option, r is the constant risk-free interest rate, T is the time in years until the maturity of the put option, S is the spot price of the underlying stock, q is the continuous dividend yield of the underlying stock and Φ is the cumulative distribution function of the standard normal distribution. Further, the parameters d_1 and d_2 are given in the following way

[2]This method is sometimes also referred to as the Black-Scholes-Merton method.

$$d_1 = \frac{\ln\left(\frac{S}{K}\right) + \left(r - q + \frac{\sigma^2}{2}\right)T}{\sigma\sqrt{T}}$$

and

$$d_2 = d_1 - \sigma\sqrt{T}$$

with σ is the volatility of the stock's returns. Whenever we use the term "implied volatilities", this refers to volatility values extracted from option market quotes. In other words, with a certain algorithm it is possible to determine the applied volatility for market option prices with this formula. The continuous dividend yield can also be extracted from the option market price due to the so-called call put parity. This parity states that, if a put and a call option have the same maturity, the same underlying stock and the same strike, then the put price plus the spot price is equal to the call price plus the discounted strike and the discounted dividend payments of the underlying stock until maturity. If this relation is violated, then an arbitrage yield is possible. The call put parity is given by the following formula

$$p + S = c + Ke^{-rT} + D,$$

with D being the discounted dividends of the stock until maturity. It is worth to notice, that we are not only able to extract implied volatilities and implied dividends but also precise dividend forecast, if enough option market data are available.

Pricing American digital options with a closed-form solution

Although, many closed-form solutions for different option types exist, there is no closed-form solution available for our pricing problem. Nevertheless, a closed-form solution for European digital option exists and the price for a put option can be calculated via the formula

$$p = \exp(-rT)\Phi(-d_2)$$

with the parameters defined as above. In this pricing formula, the payoff is either one or zero. Thus, in order to get the proper value we have to multiply this formula with $(1 - R) * nominal$ where R is the recovery rate and *nominal* the amount invested in the CDS contract. One could argue that this gives us a solid approximation with very small computational time, but we use a more accurate method since this method is only applicable to European digital options. We believe that especially with the high payment at exercise, we need to be able to model the time of exercise more precisely than to assume the exercise to happen at maturity.

3.3.2 Monte-Carlo Simulation

Stanislaw Ulam, Nicholas Metropolis and John von Neumann mainly invented the Monte-Carlo simulation, while they were partly working on the nuclear weapon project in the Los Alamos National Laboratory in the 1940s. The name to that method was given by Metropolis, who named it after the Monte Carlo Casino in Monte Carlo where Ulam used to gamble quiet often.

The Monte-Carlo simulation is a very usefully tool, because all options, no matter how exotic they are, can easily be priced with this method. The approach itself is rather simple. The future path of the asset price is simulated many times and then the present value of the option for each is path is calculated. In general, the following simulation is used for the share price

$$S_t = S_{t-\Delta t} \exp\left(\left(r - q - \frac{\sigma^2}{2} \right) \Delta t + \sigma \sqrt{\Delta t} \epsilon \right),$$

where $\epsilon \sim \mathcal{N}(0, 1)$, r the risk-free interest rate, q the dividend rate, σ^2 the volatility of the share and $\Delta t = \frac{T}{N}$ with N the number of time steps until maturity. Then, each path is evaluated at maturity and finally discounted to the pricing date. Then, the option price is the average over the (simulated) present value of the paths. Due to the fact that the approach is based on a simulation, the estimated price is always affected by an error, which is also known as the "Monte-Carlo error". This model is useful to gather a first idea of the option price, but if other methods are available, they usually lead to more trustworthy prices. Nevertheless, for some options a valuation with the Monte-Carlo simulation is the only available pricing approach such as Asian options, where the payoff is determined between the strike and the average stock price.

There also exits a specification of the Monte-Carlo simulation, which is extremely powerful for options with the right of execution before maturity. This model is the Longstaff-Schwartz model. Within this model at each step of the path, where the option is in the money, it is evaluated by a regression that determines whether it is better to execute at this time-step or to prolong the option. Thus, for each path the optimal execution time point is determined. Then, the average over all discounted paths is the value of the option.

Pricing American digital options with Monte-Carlo Simulation
We will not apply this method due to the Monte-Carlo error and the fact that we are able to evaluate trust worthier prices with another approach. Nevertheless, there is always the possibility to apply a Monte-Carlo simulation. Then, we simulate the path several times L with the stochastic model as mentioned above and remember each path's minimum spot η_i as well as the time step τ_i of this minimum. Then, the value of each path ρ_i is given by

$$\rho_i = \eta_i \exp(-\tau_i r)$$

if $\eta_i < S$ and zero otherwise. The option is out-of-the-money at the beginning and since we evaluate a put option with a strike below the spot S, we know that the value of paths with a minimum higher than S has to be zero. Further, we define for all paths i

$$\xi_i = \rho_i * payout$$

if $\eta_i \leq K$ and zero otherwise i.e. ξ_i is the value of the path i at the pricing date. Then, we are able to gather the price of the option, in dependence of the strike K, with

$$p(K) = \frac{1}{L} \sum_{i=1}^{L} \xi_i.$$

We lastly use the lowest η_i to find the corresponding $\widetilde{K}$ that $p(\widetilde{K}) \geq p_{CDS}$. We can repeat the approximation of $\widetilde{K}$ several times to gather a better approximation of the "proper" strike K. This approximation can lead to the desired strike, but there is always an error involved and the deviation process takes a longer time than the Crank-Nicolson method.

3.3.3 Tree Models

The basic idea of the tree models is to divide the maturity T into N time steps with $\Delta t = \frac{T}{N}$. At each time point $k\Delta t$ with $k \in \{1, \ldots, N\}$, the asset price has only several possibilities to move within a time-step Δt, see Fig. 3.3. The model assumes that the share price either drops or rises, which is the case of the binomial trees, or additionally remains at the same value, which is the case of the trinomial trees, in a

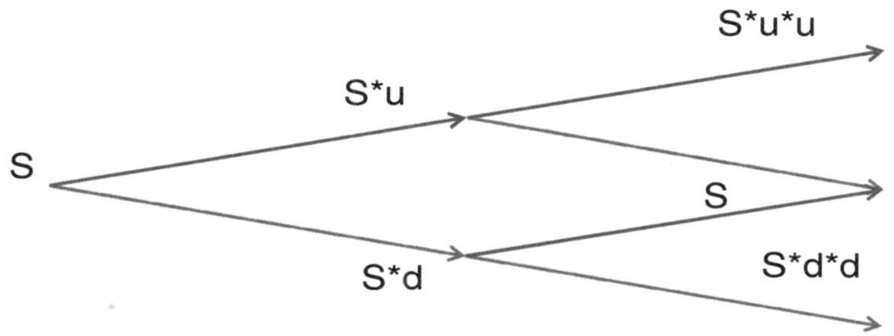

Fig. 3.3 This figure shows two steps in a binomial tree, which is the same as one step in a trinomial tree

time step Δt. Then we are able to calculate all possible states of the share price until maturity and especially the pay-off values at maturity. Given the probability of a rising, remaining or dropping of the asset price we are able to derive the expected value of the option pay-off one at $(N-1)\Delta t$, which is the time step before maturity. We only need to discount the expected value of the option to gain the options value at each asset knot at $(N-1)\Delta t$. Now we can repeat this approach of each time point until we reach $k=0$ which is the pricing date. This last value is the option price for a plain vanilla European option with a tree model.

For reasons of simplicity, we assume that the asset rises (i.e. $S_{t+\Delta t} = S_t u$) in the same amount as it falls (i.e. $S_{t+\Delta t} = S_t d = S_t \frac{1}{u}$). Thus, a trinomial is the same as two time steps on a binomial tree as we plotted in Fig. 3.3. This is the reason why we only take a look at binomial trees. It quiet easy to prove that in the case of a plain vanilla European option, the option price derived with the tree models converges towards the Black-Scholes model option price if $\Delta t \to 0$ i.e. $N \to \infty$.

Pricing American digital options with binomial trees
Concerning our pricing problem of an American digital option, we construct trees in a way that we are able to derive an adequate option price. But with the method of finite differences, we are able to calculate an option price, which is numerically more stable and converges faster to the theoretical option price. Nevertheless, we found a recursive algorithm to price an American binary option with a tree model. This algorithm is completely new as far as we know. It is in particular interesting since we are able to calculate the probability of reaching the strike as well. As we see later, this probability can also be interpreted as the probability of default (PD). We do not use this approach for the SOD deviation, because we believe that the Crank-Nicolson method, as we see later on, leads to a faster convergence and lower computational time as this one. Nevertheless, in the next few paragraphs we discuss our other pricing approach for the interested reader.

For reasons of simplicity, we assume a binomial tree and that $u = \frac{1}{d}$ with u the upward movement of the share ($S_{t+\Delta t} = S_t u$) and d the downward movements of the stock. Then probability p of a decrease in a time-step can be derived via the following formula

$$p = \frac{a-d}{u-d},$$

where

$$a = \exp((r-q)\Delta t), u = \exp\left(-\sigma\sqrt{\Delta t}\right) \text{and}\, d = \frac{1}{u}$$

with r the risk-free interest rate, q the dividend of the asset and σ^2 is the volatility of the underlying. The probability of an increase in the share value is then given via $1-p$, since there are only two ways the share can move. The discussion of the proper volatility is outlined in Sect. 3.3, but it is sufficient for now, that a proper volatility is available. It is also worth to mention that the applied volatility also depends on the strike, i.e. the volatility changes with a different strike.

As mentioned, we want to find the strike to a given option price. We apply an algorithm based on the bisectional as well as the Newton method. We apply the same approach for the determination of the strike. The first two strikes are to be chosen in a way that the proper strike lies in their interval. For the upper strike, a guess close to one in terms of moneyness and a guess close to zero are appropriate. We assume the strike to be equal to an asset knot. Otherwise, the procedure is nearly the same. If the strike is not equal to a knot, we take the next higher knot as the higher strike and the next lower knot as the lower strike. Then both option prices are determined for both strikes and finally the option price for the real strike is evaluated with an interpolation between the other two strikes.

Let us assume we have an adequate strike as well as a corresponding volatility. Furthermore, we presume that the strike is equal to an asset knot, meaning there is a $z \in \{1, \ldots, N\}$ so that $strike = Sd^z$, where S is the spot asset price at the pricing date. With the volatility as well as with the number of time steps N, we derive all possible asset prices—$(N+1)$ knots—at maturity as well as the probability of each knot being reached. We gain with our notation

$$knot_k = Sd^{N-k}u^k$$

for $k \in \{0, 1, \ldots, N\}$ and their corresponding probability

$$P(S_T = knot_k) = \binom{N}{k} p^{N-k}(1-p)^k.$$

Thus, we can determine the probability that the asset price at maturity is below a certain knot k as follows

$$P_k := P(S_T \leq knot_k) = \sum_{i=0}^{k} \binom{N}{i} p^{N-i}(1-p)^i.$$

On the one hand, the higher the number of steps N, the narrower is the asset (knots-) grid and the approximation of the strike improves. On the other hand, the calculation of the binomial coefficient easily gets very time consuming and resources intensive. Since we have an assumption about the PD which corresponds in our model to the probability of a strike hit, we can find a factor k in such way that

$$\hat{k} = k(\sigma, N) := \max(k\epsilon\{0, 1, \ldots, N\} | P_k \leq PD).$$

That is of course only applicable to European options, because it does not involve the movements, where the share price drops below the strike but raises above the strike until maturity. In our idea, this path would lead to a default but it is not used for the determination of the probability. We define

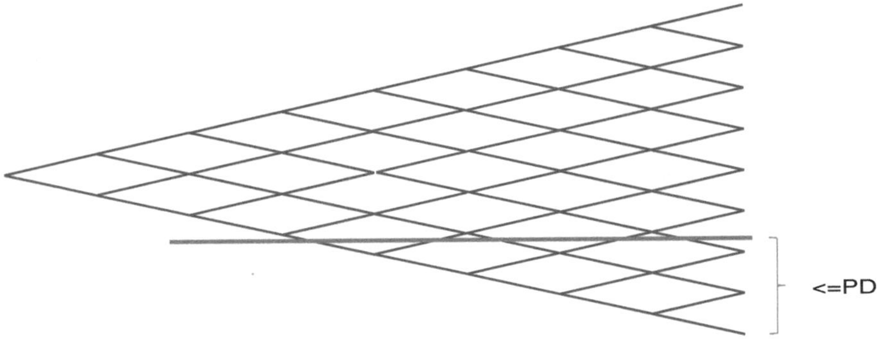

Fig. 3.4 This figure displays a binomial tree with eight time steps ($n = 8$) and at least four steps until the strike is reached ($l = 4$)

$$l = \min_{l \in \{1,\dots,N\}} \left(S_0 * d^l \leq K\right)$$

as the minimum number of down-steps until the strike is hit. In Fig. 3.4 we seen an example where $n = 8$ and $l = 4$ meaning, that in this case of 8 time steps, at least four more downward than upward movements are needed in order to reach the strike.

With the knowledge about the number of steps until the strike we can derive the option price. Consider that our option has an American exercise style as well as a fixed payment, i.e. the option gets exercised as soon as the strike is hit. The price of the option will depend on the number of time steps N, on the minimum number of steps l and the volatility σ^2. We define

$$s := \left\lfloor \frac{N-l}{2} \right\rfloor$$

as the number of up-movements that are allowed before the last or lth down-movement is done. For reasons of simplicity we further define

$$\xi := \exp(-r\Delta t), \lambda := \xi * p \text{ and } \tau := \xi^2 p(1-p).$$

With $P(l,N)$ defined as the option price with N time steps and a minimum step of l before the strike is reached, the following relation can easily be derived

$$P(l,N) = \xi p P(l-1, N-1) + \xi(1-p)P(l+1, N),$$

assuming the same strike respectively the same applied volatility. Then, we are able to determine the option price $P(l,N)$ as the following polynomial

$$P(l,N) = nominal * (1-R)\lambda^l \sum_{i=0}^{s} a_{i,l}\tau^i,$$

with

$$a_{0,l} = 1 \text{ and } a_{i,l} = \sum_{r=2}^{l+1} a_{i-1,r}.$$

This formula might appear a bit strange at the first moment, but it gets clear if one looks at $s = 0$ for instance. From $s = 0$ we gather that $n - l = 0$ or $n - l = 1$, i.e. the strike is the very last knot or even the knot before and there is only one way to get to that knot namely by going downwards all the time. If $s = 1$ then, until hitting the strike, the path is allowed to go one up movement i.e.

$$a_{1,l} = \sum_{r=2}^{l+1} a_{0,r} = l.$$

For $s = 2$ the path is allowed to use two up movements' and then

$$a_{2,l} = \sum_{r=2}^{l+1} r = \frac{1}{2}(l^2 + 3l)$$

and so on. We tried to find a closer form for the parameters $a_{i,l}$ and are very glad if someone else finds a better solution. Nevertheless, these parameters can easily be programmed we just need to be careful with the "lower ranks" since one needs more of them than it seems in the first place. Until now, we assumed a fixed strike, i.e. the strike, is the same over the whole time until maturity.

3.3.4 Finite Differences

The basic idea of the finite difference is to approximate the differential equation with a numeric approach as mentioned in the beginning of this chapter. There are mainly two different approaches within the finite difference approach. On the one hand, there is the implicit finite differences method, which is numerically stable, but does not converge as fast to the theoretical option price. On the other hand, there is the explicit finite differences method, which is not always numerically stable but convergences rather fast to the theoretical price. Furthermore, the explicit finite differences method is equivalent to the trinomial tree approach as discussed in the earlier section. In order to combine the advantages of both methods, the Crank-Nicolson method, a combination of explicit and implicit, has become very popular.

Pricing American digital options with the Crank-Nicolson approach
Concerning our pricing problem, we use the Crank-Nicolson approach with an adjusted payoff as described below. Then, we use an algorithm to fit the option price via altering the strike and the applied volatility with it. Because the finite differences lead to very solid results, we assume that this result is the most solid price given the least time to evaluate and a numerically stable approach without any simulation errors as in the Monte-Carlo simulation.

The approach of the finite differences method is to build a grid (i,j), where i denotes the time and j the spot price. In other words, we divide the time to maturity in N the number of time steps as in the tree models, i.e. $i = i\Delta t = i\frac{T}{N}$. Additionally we divide the possible asset price range into M the number of asset steps, i.e. $j = j\Delta S = j\frac{S_{\max}}{M}$ with $S_{\max}$ is the maximum value of the spot in that way, that the put value is zero at all time. We use the following approximation $S_{\max} = S + 3\sigma\sqrt{T}$, which is a rather standard assumption for pricing put options with finite differences. We denote the put value $f_{i,j}$ at the grid point (i,j) and we further do know, so conditions

$$f_{i,M} = 0 \,\text{for all}\, i \in \{0, 1, \ldots, N\},$$

$$f_{N,j} = 0 \,\text{if}\, j\Delta S > K$$

and

$$f_{N,j} = (1 - R) * \mathit{nominal} \,\text{if}\, j\Delta S \leq K$$

where R is the recovery rate. Since we deal with an American digital option i.e. the pay-off does not depend on the moneyness

$$f_{i,j} = (1 - R) * \mathit{nominal} \,\text{if}\, j\Delta S \leq K \,\text{for all}\, i \in \{0, 1, \ldots, N\}.$$

The numerical approximations of the derivative for any function f is done in the following form

$$\frac{\delta f}{\delta x} = \frac{f(x + \mathrm{h}) - f(x)}{\mathrm{h}},$$

where $h > 0$. To gain the theoretical deviation, we need to construct the limit for $h \to 0$. Then we rewrite the derivative for our purpose in the following way

$$\frac{\delta f}{\delta S} = \frac{f_{i,j+1} - f_{i,j}}{\Delta S}$$

or

$$\frac{\delta f}{\delta S} = \frac{f_{i,j} - f_{i,j-1}}{\Delta S}.$$

The same approach can also be done to the second derivative as well as to the derivative with respect to the time. Then, all finite difference approaches follow directly, if all equations are used to approximate the original differential equation

$$\frac{\delta f}{\delta t} + (r - q)S\frac{\delta f}{\delta S} + \frac{1}{2}\sigma^2 S^2 \frac{\delta^2 f}{\delta S^2} = rf.$$

Finally, with all mandatory parameters calculated, we are able to derive an American digital put option price. The mandatory parameters can be found in the books we mentioned earlier.

3.3.5 Applied Volatilities

For our research we apply volatilities, which we extract from implied volatilities from deep-out-of-the money options, meaning from options with moneyness far below one. The moneyness is defined as follows

$$\text{moneyness} = \frac{\text{strike}}{\text{spot price}}.$$

It might be the case that for different entities the strike is lower than the lowest moneyness available. In this case, we have to assume a model for the extrapolation of the volatility surface. We apply a cubic spline extrapolation. It can be argued that especially for shorter maturities the extrapolation by Bates (1996) is a better approach, but as we will see, our volatility data for a maturity shorter than one year is absolutely adequate. For moneyness in between two grid points, we apply a cubic spline interpolation.

3.4 Data Set

For this paper we looked at twenty-two German corporations that are highly liquid and, apart from Porsche, all corporations are either members of the DAX or the MDAX. Such selection of corporations guarantees a rather high degree of diversification. These entities include Allianz, BASF, BMW, Commerzbank, Continental, Deutsche Bank, Daimler, Deutsche Post, Deutsche Telekom, E.ON, HeidelbergerCement, Henkel, Hannover Re, Linde, Metro, Munich RE, Porsche,

RWE, Siemens, ThyssenKrupp, TUI and Volkswagen. We gathered the CDS data, which are constant maturity contracts as mentioned in Chap. 2, on each underlying market spreads for the maturities of six months, one and two years. Furthermore, we gained the underlying's implied volatility surfaces from iVolatility[3] with the maturities shorter than three years. The implied volatilities are based on plain vanilla American options. This is of great importance for us, since we evaluate digital options with an American exercise style. The grid of the volatilities ranges from a moneyness of 0.4 up to 1 for each maturity. The relevant time interval is the month January 2013, i.e. we are able to derive an SOD on twenty-two days for twenty-two different corporations with three different maturities and two different prices (clean vs. dirty), which leads us to 2904 points of observation.

3.5 Results

The results are compactly displayed in Table 3.1 for the six-month maturity, in Table 3.2 for the one-year maturity and in Table 3.3 for the two-year maturity. At the first glimpse the strike of default (SOD) decreases on average with time to maturity as expected. On average the SOD based on the dirty CDS-option prices falls from 0.511 for the six months maturity to 0.434 for the one-year maturity and finally to 0.369 for the two-year maturity. For the clean CDS-option prices, the SOD drops from 0.329 for six months to 0.286 for one year and finally to 0.256 for two years. This tendency confirms our intuitive assumption, because we assume that the longer the maturity the more the share price may fall until an actual default occurs. For example, a loss of fifty per cent of stock value within two years may not lead to a default but the same scenario within six month is a totally different scenario. However, in some rare cases the SOD increases during a longer maturity but we will get to this later.

Before we continue, we need to outline some relations. First, the price of a put option decreases when the strike decreases, if all other parameters stay the same. This is the case, because in such situation it is less likely that the share price reaches the strike, i.e. the probability that the option will be exercised drops. If we think of the option price as the discounted expected value, this fact gets even more intuitive. Secondly, the dirty CDS-option price is greater or equal than the clean CDS-option price. This relation is trivial, since the dirty CDS-option price is equal to the clean CDS-option price plus the accrued interest, which cannot be negative. Therefore, we also presume that the SOD based on the dirty CDS-option price is higher than the SOD based on the clean CDS-option price. This presumption is proven by the data. If we again consider the deviation of the premium leg, we can state that if the maturity increases, so does the number of (possible) coupon dates. Therefore, the rate between the accrued interests and the clean CDS-option price drops. Thus,

[3]For further information take a look at www.ivolatility.com.

Table 3.1 In this table the mean and the standard deviation (in brackets) of the dirty and clean six months SOD are shown for each company

6 month maturity	Strike of default		Implied volatility		CDS (in bps)	
	Dirty	Clean	Dirty	Clean	Market spread	Deal spread
Allianz	0.531 (0.085)	0.249 (0.017)	0.316 (0.021)	0.393 (0.028)	11.338 (4.075)	25
BASF	0.552 (0.072)	0.33 (0.047)	0.326 (0.046)	0.447 (0.054)	6.636 (1.476)	25
BMW	0.519 (0.047)	0.329 (0.021)	0.357 (0.022)	0.447 (0.019)	8.911 (1.503)	25
Commerzbank	0.218 (0.079)	0.069 (0.011)	0.895 (0.117)	1.081 (0.054)	14.524 (4.545)	50
Continental	0.473 (0.067)	0.327 (0.028)	0.406 (0.045)	0.451 (0.029)	30.145 (3.381)	25
Deutsche Bank	0.391 (0.057)	0.222 (0.022)	0.502 (0.043)	0.605 (0.042)	9.806 (5.019)	25
Daimler	0.532 (0.053)	0.307 (0.031)	0.345 (0.028)	0.476 (0.034)	15.896 (1.121)	25
Deutsche Post	0.531 (0.085)	0.249 (0.017)	0.348 (0.062)	0.558 (0.025)	6.195 (0.26)	25
Deutsche Telekom	0.587 (0.058)	0.451 (0.015)	0.293 (0.034)	0.321 (0.011)	14.912 (1.479)	25
E.ON	0.577 (0.039)	0.466 (0.019)	0.302 (0.015)	0.307 (0.011)	11.388 (1.223)	25
HeidelbergerCement	0.479 (0.045)	0.344 (0.016)	0.398 (0.021)	0.43 (0.012)	27.531 (5.511)	25
Henkel	0.574 (0.05)	0.343 (0.03)	0.305 (0.025)	0.431 (0.029)	8.832 (1.289)	25
Hannover Re	0.563 (0.044)	0.397 (0.015)	0.315 (0.02)	0.372 (0.009)	13.33 (4.871)	25
Linde	0.597 (0.039)	0.431 (0.014)	0.284 (0.014)	0.339 (0.008)	9.707 (0.652)	25
Metro	0.601 (0.049)	0.491 (0.029)	0.281 (0.023)	0.287 (0.019)	24.86 (4.074)	25
Munich RE	0.548 (0.055)	0.357 (0.033)	0.329 (0.029)	0.417 (0.031)	10.276 (3.268)	25
Porsche	0.488 (0.018)	0.378 (0.011)	0.389 (0.015)	0.394 (0.018)	8.115 (1.012)	25
RWE	0.553 (0.052)	0.354 (0.043)	0.324 (0.027)	0.419 (0.044)	13.158 (2.003)	25
Siemens	0.583 (0.04)	0.412 (0.007)	0.296 (0.016)	0.357 (0.004)	7.554 (1.123)	25
ThyssenKrupp	0.445 (0.068)	0.241 (0.021)	0.436 (0.048)	0.573 (0.027)	28.135 (6.752)	25

(continued)

Table 3.1 (continued)

6 month maturity	Strike of default		Implied volatility		CDS (in bps)	
	Dirty	Clean	Dirty	Clean	Market spread	Deal spread
TUI	0.412 (0.084)	0.183 (0.048)	0.546 (0.082)	0.702 (0.103)	53.601 (6.375)	50
Volkswagen	0.492 (0.072)	0.312 (0.037)	0.386 (0.051)	0.47 (0.045)	10.387 (1.184)	25
Mean	0.511 (0.057)	0.329 (0.024)	0.381 (0.037)	0.467 (0.03)	15.693 (11.39)	

In the last two columns we find the applied volatility and the market spreads

Table 3.2 In this table, the mean and the standard deviation (in brackets) of the dirty and clean one year SOD are shown for each company

1 year maturity	Strike of default		Implied volatility		CDS (in bps)	
	Dirty	Clean	Dirty	Clean	Market spread	Deal spread
Allianz	0.472 (0.057)	0.273 (0.031)	0.335 (0.019)	0.34 (0.019)	15.705 (5.302)	25
BASF	0.429 (0.076)	0.255 (0.039)	0.352 (0.048)	0.424 (0.041)	6.898 (1.531)	25
BMW	0.423 (0.041)	0.313 (0.016)	0.355 (0.017)	0.361 (0.011)	12.523 (0.721)	25
Commerzbank	0.188 (0.042)	0.066 (0.02)	0.736 (0.061)	0.851 (0.069)	34.853 (4.818)	50
Continental	0.447 (0.055)	0.294 (0.042)	0.383 (0.031)	0.414 (0.046)	42.569 (2.523)	50
Deutsche Bank	0.313 (0.045)	0.185 (0.015)	0.469 (0.028)	0.516 (0.023)	13.44 (3.614)	25
Daimler	0.436 (0.048)	0.304 (0.025)	0.344 (0.023)	0.37 (0.021)	18.217 (1.262)	25
Deutsche Post	0.472 (0.057)	0.273 (0.031)	0.313 (0.029)	0.405 (0.038)	7.429 (0.322)	25
Deutsche Telekom	0.539 (0.044)	0.431 (0.02)	0.261 (0.021)	0.267 (0.013)	20.705 (1.471)	25
E.ON	0.497 (0.031)	0.396 (0.015)	0.292 (0.009)	0.292 (0.009)	16.253 (0.888)	25
HeidelbergerCement	0.43 (0.032)	0.281 (0.036)	0.4 (0.013)	0.427 (0.041)	50.483 (10.087)	50
Henkel	0.467 (0.031)	0.32 (0.017)	0.317 (0.01)	0.356 (0.017)	9.576 (1.845)	25
Hannover Re	0.484 (0.065)	0.238 (0.018)	0.348 (0.034)	0.475 (0.02)	19.305 (5.781)	50
Linde	0.484 (0.04)	0.366 (0.012)	0.303 (0.015)	0.317 (0.008)	10.802 (0.86)	25

(continued)

Table 3.2 (continued)

1 year maturity	Strike of default		Implied volatility		CDS (in bps)	
	Dirty	Clean	Dirty	Clean	Market spread	Deal spread
Metro	0.551 (0.058)	0.427 (0.037)	0.29 (0.027)	0.291 (0.025)	31.033 (5.167)	50
Munich RE	0.423 (0.055)	0.237 (0.028)	0.356 (0.032)	0.451 (0.047)	11.677 (3.581)	25
Porsche	0.385 (0.023)	0.276 (0.013)	0.391 (0.009)	0.4 (0.017)	11.682 (0.983)	25
RWE	0.455 (0.039)	0.353 (0.019)	0.327 (0.015)	0.325 (0.013)	16.94 (2.909)	25
Siemens	0.479 (0.032)	0.349 (0.024)	0.307 (0.012)	0.331 (0.023)	10.025 (0.838)	25
ThyssenKrupp	0.44 (0.047)	0.274 (0.024)	0.389 (0.019)	0.433 (0.029)	51.85 (20.887)	50
TUI	0.41 (0.072)	0.194 (0.041)	0.503 (0.048)	0.587 (0.066)	80.139 (9.674)	100
Volkswagen	0.33 (0.056)	0.18 (0.036)	0.451 (0.052)	0.53 (0.064)	13.842 (1.475)	25
Mean	0.434 (0.048)	0.286 (0.025)	0.374 (0.026)	0.417 (0.03)	22.998 (19.018)	

In the last two columns we find the applied volatility and the market spreads

Table 3.3 In this table, the mean and the standard deviation (in brackets) of the dirty and clean two-year SODs is shown for each company

2 year maturity	Strike of default		Implied volatility		CDS (in bps)	
	Dirty	Clean	Dirty	Clean	Market spread	Deal spread
Allianz	0.383 (0.033)	0.266 (0.021)	0.354 (0.023)	0.366 (0.025)	28.191 (5.238)	25
BASF	0.352 (0.05)	0.253 (0.03)	0.32 (0.024)	0.332 (0.025)	15.546 (1.325)	25
BMW	0.303 (0.041)	0.214 (0.021)	0.361 (0.019)	0.369 (0.019)	31.539 (1.208)	25
Commerzbank	0.324 (0.057)	0.191 (0.044)	0.47 (0.033)	0.477 (0.058)	50.085 (5.668)	100
Continental	0.427 (0.058)	0.27 (0.023)	0.367 (0.02)	0.383 (0.02)	82.512 (4.314)	100
Deutsche Bank	0.306 (0.045)	0.192 (0.016)	0.41 (0.021)	0.427 (0.018)	28.789 (6.517)	50
Daimler	0.393 (0.046)	0.278 (0.021)	0.331 (0.017)	0.34 (0.015)	39.384 (1.617)	50
Deutsche Post	0.383 (0.033)	0.266 (0.021)	0.296 (0.012)	0.322 (0.017)	17.923 (0.237)	25

(continued)

Table 3.3 (continued)

2 year maturity	Strike of default		Implied volatility		CDS (in bps)	
	Dirty	Clean	Dirty	Clean	Market spread	Deal spread
Deutsche Telekom	0.556 (0.04)	0.45 (0.015)	0.217 (0.01)	0.219 (0.008)	37.869 (1.711)	50
E.ON	0.442 (0.036)	0.357 (0.018)	0.255 (0.01)	0.255 (0.01)	35.507 (0.648)	25
HeidelbergerCement	0.377 (0.042)	0.219 (0.036)	0.414 (0.02)	0.44 (0.045)	95.376 (10.682)	100
Henkel	0.371 (0.028)	0.276 (0.019)	0.305 (0.012)	0.314 (0.016)	18.296 (1.678)	25
Hannover Re	0.259 (0.06)	0.122 (0.014)	0.462 (0.041)	0.53 (0.022)	34.956 (7.54)	50
Linde	0.397 (0.035)	0.313 (0.023)	0.285 (0.011)	0.285 (0.015)	20.383 (0.667)	25
Metro	0.517 (0.069)	0.378 (0.038)	0.293 (0.027)	0.294 (0.026)	72.88 (5.254)	100
Munich RE	0.351 (0.056)	0.237 (0.035)	0.322 (0.032)	0.349 (0.033)	22.279 (3.664)	25
Porsche	0.27 (0.031)	0.191 (0.014)	0.391 (0.016)	0.394 (0.015)	22.717 (1.016)	25
RWE	0.421 (0.035)	0.336 (0.018)	0.268 (0.01)	0.268 (0.011)	33.83 (3.292)	25
Siemens	0.423 (0.027)	0.337 (0.009)	0.268 (0.004)	0.267 (0.005)	19.883 (1.159)	25
ThyssenKrupp	0.429 (0.047)	0.268 (0.016)	0.365 (0.011)	0.385 (0.014)	95.444 (6.54)	100
TUI	0.278 (0.056)	0.134 (0.02)	0.523 (0.034)	0.56 (0.033)	160.992 (11.622)	100
Volkswagen	0.159 (0.042)	0.086 (0.024)	0.534 (0.058)	0.568 (0.058)	32.371 (1.286)	25
Mean	0.369 (0.044)	0.256 (0.022)	0.355 (0.021)	0.37 (0.023)	45.307 (35.117)	

In the last two columns we find the applied volatility and the market spreads

we presume the difference between the dirty and the clean SOD to decrease with an increase in maturity. This presumption is also proven, by the data as we observe that on average, the gap between dirty and clean SOD diminishes with an increase in maturity. It is about 0.182 for the six-month maturity, 0.148 for the one-year maturity and 0.113 for the two-year maturity. To briefly recapture, the unit of the SOD is moneyness, i.e. if the dirty SOD is about 0.2 higher that means that the actual dirty strike is 0.2**spot* higher than the clean strike.

Furthermore, we notice that the standard deviation of the dirty SOD is higher than the standard deviation of the clean SOD. On average, the standard deviation of the dirty SOD does decrease with time (0.057, 0.048 and 0.044), which is not entirely surprising since the ratio of the accrued interest to the clean CDS price decreases due to the higher number of coupon dates. This observation is not that surprising since the dirty CDS price already rises by construction by about 1/12**deal spread* in our data set. For example, if we consider the market spread to be constant over the time interval, then the standard deviation of the clean CDS-option price would be close to zero—given minor movements due to the interest rate. In the same case, the dirty CDS-option price rises by 1/12**deal spread* and with this movement the dirty SOD also changes. Therefore, the standard deviation of the dirty SOD has to be higher than the standard deviation of the clean SOD. The changes on the volatility surface impact both CDS-option prices to the same extent.

In the next step, we use a cubic spline interpolation to gain a smooth function, which we refer to as the "SOD function", for each valuation date. A spline interpolation is a method to gain a function, if only a few grid points are given. This function obviously runs through each grid point. Interpolation methods find functions between grid points and these partial functions only meet at the grid points. In the case of a cubic spline interpolation, the partial functions are quadratic polynomials and their first and second deviations on the grid points are the same, which delivers a very smooth function. In our case, we have three grid points namely the six months SOD, the one-year SOD and the two-year SOD. Deriving the SOD function we are able to estimate the SOD for maturities in between our grid points, e.g. for ten months. It is reasonable to argue, that an interpolation—especially a cubic spline interpolation—with only three grid points does not make a lot sense. Unfortunately, we are not able to gather more grid points, since the volatility surfaces only last until a maturity of three years and we have only got three CDS maturities within three years. This is, because the time to maturity of a three year CDS is always a bit higher than 3.0, since the CDS quote is from a constant maturity CDS contract, and therefore we have to extrapolate the volatility surface in the time direction and in the strike direction, i.e. with no actual valid grid point. An extrapolation in more than one direction would lead to values, which are too vague. At last, we also extrapolated the SOD function to gain functions with a maturity from six months to thirty months. For the extrapolation, we just continue the last respectively first partial functions. This is clearly a discuss-worthy topic, but we want to keep the model as simple as possible.

In Fig. 3.5 we see the SOD functions for each day in our sample for Allianz based on the dirty CDS-option price. Here, it seems that the SOD functions contain a convex form. Further, we observe that with each day the function shifts a bit upwards. This phenomenon is based on the increase of the accrued interest. In Fig. 3.6 we also see a SOD function for Allianz, but this time the SOD function is based on the clean CDS-option prices. In this figure, the SOD functions seem to not only upwards but also downwards shift in between the days. The SOD function movements seem to response more sensitively to impacts on the implied volatility surface and the CDS spread on the particular valuation date. Nevertheless, a general tendency towards a gain the clean SOD over time is noticeable. In the case of the clean SOD-function, the functions seem to be of a concave form. This means, that

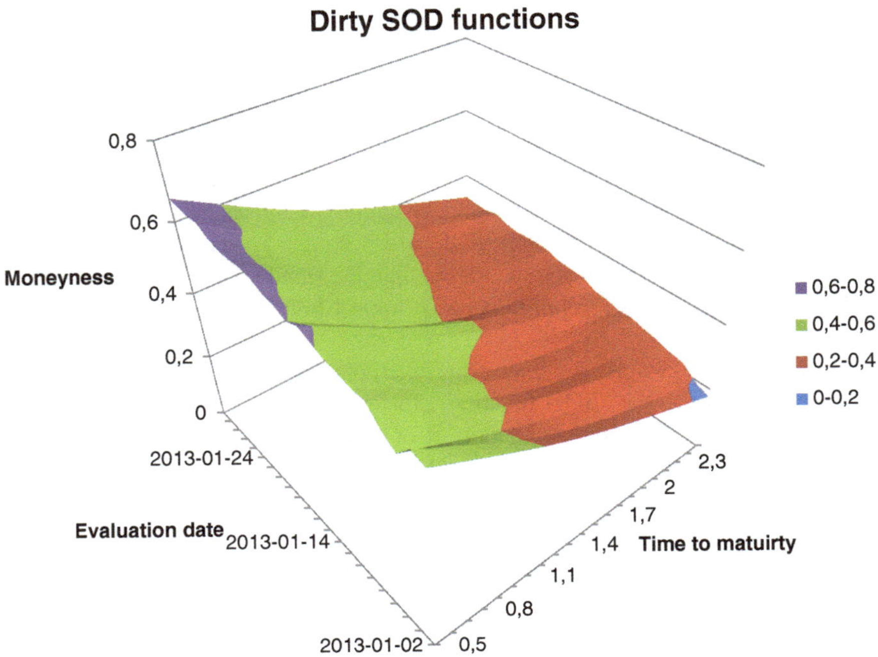

Fig. 3.5 This graph displays the dirty SOD functions of the Allianz for all working days in the January 2013

we are unfortunately not able to tell right from the beginning whether the SOD function contains a convex or concave form. Without going into each result, we mainly find that the clean SOD functions are most often convex and the dirty SOD functions are most often concave. The reason for that kind of behaviour probably is the accrued interest, which absorbs some movements of the market spread respectively some movements of the implied volatility surface.

As the results show, the volatility surface plays the most important role in the determination of the SOD. Obviously, the CDS market spread and especially the deal spread also play an important role, but the structure of the volatility is very important as we observe in Figs. 3.7 and 3.8. In Fig. 3.7 the straight line represents the SOD function, where we can determine the SOD for any ttm, and the dotted lines are the corresponding applied volatilities to the SOD and ttm. These applied volatilities are also interpolated or extrapolated based on the applied volatilities for the grid points. The red lines belong to Commerzbank whereas the blue lines belong to Metro. On the one hand, we note that the volatility for Metro is very flat and remains at about 40 % for the whole time period, which results in a monotonic decreasing SOD function as we expected. On the other hand, by the example of Commerzbank we observe that the volatility begins with very high values for shorter maturities and rapidly drops for longer maturity. The corresponding dirty SOD function increases strongly monotonic. Interpreting these numbers, their type

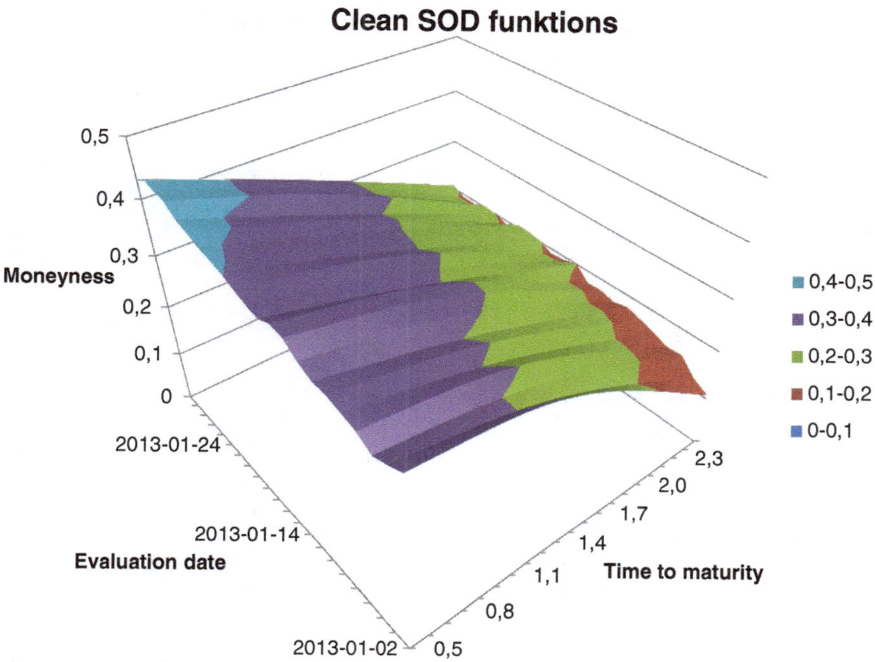

Fig. 3.6 This graph displays the clean SOD functions of the Allianz for all working days in the January 2013

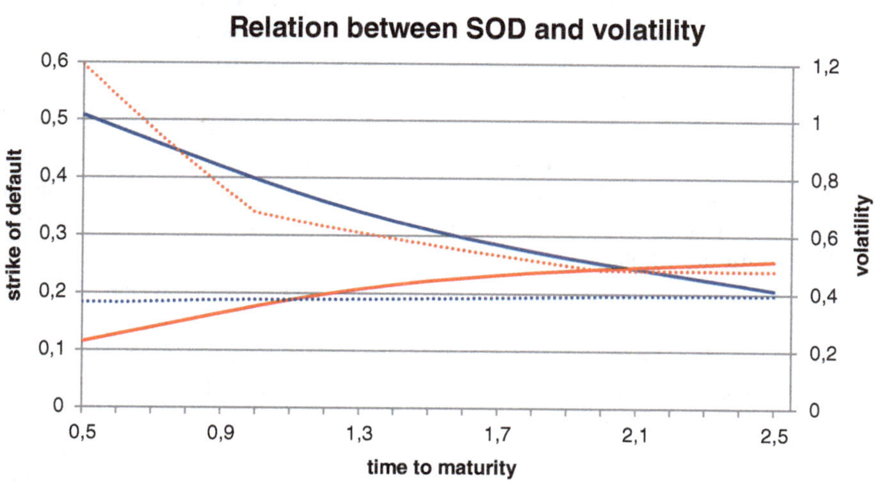

Fig. 3.7 The dirty SOD function (*straight line*) and their related volatility (*dotted line*) against the time of maturity of Commerzbank (*red lines*) and Metro (*blue lines*) on 2013-01-02. We observe that the structure of the SOD function depends deeply on the structure of the volatility surface

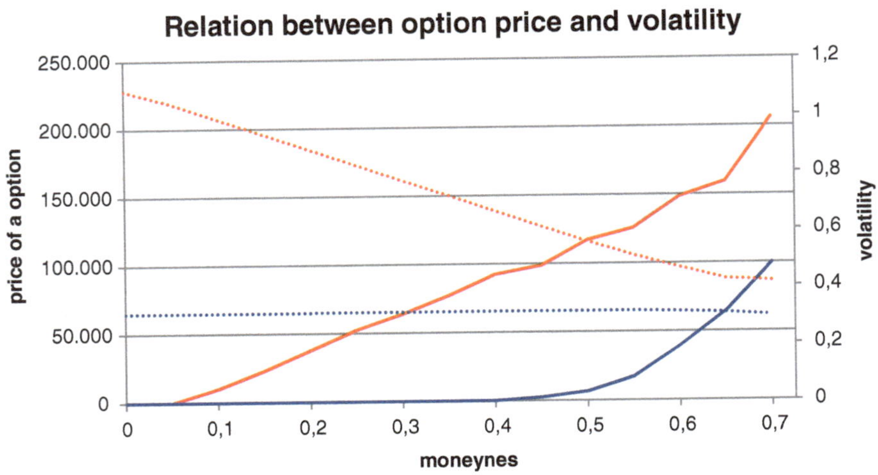

Fig. 3.8 The price of the American digital option (*straight line*) of a CDS with a security of one million euros and its applied volatility (*dotted lines*) of Commerzbank (*red lines*) and Metro (*blue lines*) for the one-year CDS data on 2013-01-02. We observe that with a more or less constant volatility, the put option price decreases rapidly if the strike decreases

of structure of the SOD function does not make any sense. In particular, the Commerzbank defaults at a barrier of e.g. 0.2 within a year—however in the first six months the bank does not default until the barrier of about 0.11 is reached. In the case of Commerzbank, each SOD is below 0.4, which is the lower boundary of the available implied volatility surface. Therefore, the applied volatilities of all SODs are extrapolated. Thus, it is worth debating, whether the cubic spline extrapolation is a good fit. On a random basis—but always with a decreasing SOD-function—, we use different methods to gather volatilities below a moneyness of 0.4. We apply other methods namely, a linear extrapolation and the fixing of the volatility with the volatility at the lowest moneyness available (0.4 moneyness). The results of this simple back testing were the same, i.e. a decreasing SOD function. Therefore in the case of a decreasing SOD function, we suggest, to apply the most conservative SOD value for the whole period. This implies a flat SOD function at all times with $SOD = SOD_{highest}$, where $SOD_{highest}$ is the highest SOD value at the valuation date.

In Fig. 3.8 we monitor the option prices (straight lines) and the applied volatilities (dotted lines) on 2013-01-02. The one-year CDS market data for Commerzbank (red lines) and Metro (blue lines) were very close on 2013-01-02. That means, the CDS-option prices (clean or dirty) were very similar. The dirty CDS-option price is about €25,000 and the clean CDS-option price is about €6.00 both for a CDS nominal of €1,000,000. Therefore, only the shape of the implied volatility surface and its value determine the SOD. Due to the different shapes of the implied or extrapolated volatility surfaces, the price of the American digital option drops either faster or slower. Without looking at the data, most people would presume Commerzbank being the company involving a greater risk and hence

Table 3.4 This table shows the average probability of default until maturity and the average strike of default (dirty) in January 2013 (i.e. 22 observations per figure)

	6 Month		1 Year		2 Year	
	Average PD (%)	Average SOD	Average PD (%)	Average SOD	Average PD (%)	Average SOD
Allianz	0.140	0.5625	0.330	0.4462	1.060	0.3113
BASF	0.080	0.5519	0.150	0.4293	0.590	0.3522
BMW	0.110	0.5194	0.260	0.4235	1.190	0.3034
Commerzbank	0.180	0.2178	0.730	0.1882	1.880	0.3237
Continental	0.380	0.4731	0.890	0.4467	3.080	0.427
Deutsche Bank	0.120	0.391	0.280	0.3129	1.090	0.3056
Daimler	0.200	0.5315	0.380	0.4362	1.480	0.3929
Deutsche Post	0.080	0.5307	0.160	0.472	0.680	0.3828
Deutsche Telekom	0.190	0.5875	0.440	0.5394	1.430	0.5561
E.ON	0.140	0.5768	0.340	0.4972	1.340	0.4422
HeidelbergerCement	0.350	0.4789	1.060	0.4299	3.560	0.3769
Henkel	0.110	0.574	0.200	0.4668	0.690	0.3705
Hannover Re	0.170	0.5628	0.410	0.4844	1.320	0.2589
Linde	0.120	0.5975	0.230	0.4836	0.770	0.3973
Metro	0.310	0.6005	0.650	0.5509	2.730	0.5169
Munich RE	0.130	0.5483	0.250	0.4229	0.840	0.3507
Porsche	0.100	0.4885	0.250	0.3848	0.860	0.2703
RWE	0.170	0.5533	0.360	0.4554	1.280	0.4213
Siemens	0.100	0.5835	0.210	0.4789	0.750	0.4226
ThyssenKrupp	0.360	0.4454	1.090	0.44	3.560	0.429
TUI	0.680	0.4122	1.670	0.4096	5.930	0.2777
Volkswagen	0.130	0.4921	0.290	0.3304	1.220	0.1588

should possess a higher SOD. Due to the higher volatility, the SOD for Commerzbank and the option prices are higher—thus the Commerzbank's SOD is lower than the SOD for Metro. This is a surprising result. Based on the last findings, we have to state that the SOD is not a risk measure enabling the direct comparison between any two companies. A lower SOD does not necessarily imply a stable company without any risk of default.

In Table 3.4 we present the average dirty SOD as well as the average PD for each company for all three maturities in January 2013. The deviation of the probability is the same approach as mentioned earlier in Sect. 2.3 with a constant hazard rate term structure. This table empirically proves that corporations with the same average SOD do not have the same PD and vice versa. If we consider a maturity of six months, we will observe that BASF and RWE have about the same average SOD (0.55), but the PD is nearly twice as a high for RWE as for BASF. On the other hand, BMW and Henkel have the same average PD, but the average SOD of Henkel is about 0.06 higher than the one of RWE. The same effects arise for longer maturities, e.g. for the one-year maturity of Allianz/Continental or E.ON/RWE and for two-year maturity of HeidelbergerCement/ThyssenKrupp. At last, we point out that for TUI, the company with the highest PD within two years (about 6 %), has about the same average SOD as Porsche with a relatively low average PD (about 0.9 %).

3.6 Conclusion

We are able to derive an SOD for each company. The behaviours of the SODs are plausible and we are able to determine valid estimations for an SOD. The deviation of the SOD and its theory may be rather theoretical and the assumptions are of course arguable, but we deeply believe that the SOD may serve as a valuable alternative risk measure with great flexibility and only few market data needed in comparison to the KMV model. Furthermore, the SOD function delivers a feeling about the default risk development over time.

Unfortunately, we are not able to compare any two companies simply based on their SOD alone. This is due to the volatility surface and especially its structure, which plays a major role in the determination of the SOD. Depending on the volatility surface, a lower SOD might be more likely to occur due to higher volatility. Furthermore, some results leads to the impression that the SOD rises with the maturities which of course does not make sense in the way we interpret the SOD. In such cases a flat SOD, with its highest derived value, over time would be a conservative approach.

There are several ways how to improve this approach. The use of different models for the volatility, for the derivation of the option price or even to use other options such as down-and-in put options or even plain vanilla American put options can be examined. Furthermore, one could argue that the price of the option has to be equal to the protection leg, i.e. that the actual CDS price is reconstructed.

References

G. Angelopoulus, D. Giamouridis, G. Nikolakakis, Stock return predictability of cross-market deviations in option prices and credit default swap spreads. Available at SSRN 1991179 (2012, January)

D.S. Bates, Jumps and stochastic volatility: exchange rate processes implicit in Deutsche Mark options. Rev. Finan. Stud. **9**(1), 69–107 (1996)

F. Black, M.S. Scholes, The pricing of options and corporate liabilities. J. Polit. Econ. (7), 637–654 (1973)

H. Byström, Credit default swaps and equity prices: The iTraxx CDS index market. Working Papers, Department of Economics, Lund University **24** (2005)

C. Cao, F. Yu, Z. Zhong, The information content of option-implied volatility for credit default swap valuation. J. Finan. Markets **13**(3), 321–343 (2010)

P. Carr, L. Wu, A simple robust link between American puts and credit protection. Rev. Finan. Stud. **24**(2), 473–505 (2011)

P. Carr, L. Wu, Stock options and credit default swaps: a joint framework for valuation and estimation. J. Finan. Econometrics (2009): nbp010

P. Collin-Dufresne, R. Goldstein, J. Martin, The determination of credit spread changes. J. Finance **56**(6), 2177–2207 (2001)

J. Cox, J. Ingersol Jr., S. Ross, A theory of the term structure of interest rates, 385–408 (1985)

S.L. Heston, A closed-form solution for options with stochastic volatility with applications to bond and currency options. Rev. Finan. Stud. **6**(2), 327–343 (1993)

J.C. Hull, *Options, futures, and other derivatives*, 5th edn. (Pearson Education, Harlow, England, 2012)

J.C. Hull, I. Nelken, A. White, Merton's model, credit risk, and volatility skews. J. Credit Risk **1** (1), 8–23 (2004)

R.C. Merton, On the pricing of corporate debt: The risk structure of interest rates. J. Finance **29**(2), 449–479 (1974)

M.F. Schmidt, Credit default swaps from an equity point of view. *World Finance Conference* (2014)

P. Wilmott, Paul Wilmott on quantitative finance (John Wiley & Sons, 2013)

B.Y. Zhang, H. Zhou, H. Zhu, Explaining credit default swap spreads with the equity volatility and jump risks of individual firms. Rev. Finan. Stud. **22**(12), 5099–5131 (2009)

Chapter 4
Strike of Default: Sensitivity and Times Series Analysis

Abstract In this chapter we discuss the sensitivity of the strike of default (SOD), with respect to its greatest factors of influence—the CDS market spread and the option volatility. We explore the idea of hedging a CDS protection sell with American put options against a credit event which we assume to happen once the stock price reaches the SOD. At last, we analyze portfolio investment strategies to place the earnings from CDS protection sells for at-the-money (ATM) American options. Historical data have shown that with our investment strategy we are able to gain a profit of at least 31 % in 27 months.

In this chapter we take a deeper look at the strike of default (SOD). The SOD is a synthetic risk measure for exchange-listed companies. This risk measure is derived via credit default swap (CDS) spreads and market data from traded options on the same underlying as the CDS. This strike can be seen as a barrier to the share price at which the credit and option market believe the company would collapse. This threshold is a dynamic benchmark and can be calculated at any time, as long as CDS spreads and market volatilities are available. In comparison to Moody's KMV model, which is based on a structural approach, the SOD is based purely upon market data and does not need any further information such as company's debts or even balance sheet data.

From the technical point of view, the SOD is the result of a fitting American digital option, with the implementation of interpolated volatilities from implied volatility surfaces, to an option price, which we calculate form the corresponding CDS spread. The strike of the corresponding American digital option, which we interpreted as the stock price where the company would presumable crash, is defined as the SOD. While deviation and some behaviours of the SOD already have been discussed in Schmidt (2014a), we would like to concentrate in more detail on the sensitivity of the SOD as well as a time series study. In the time series study we analyse whether the SOD has been reached and whether the SOD can used to

This chapter is a working paper by Schmidt. See Schmidt (2014a)—"Strike of default: Sensitivity and time series analysis". This paper is accepted at the World Finance Conference in Singapore in December 2014.

M. Schmidt, *Pricing and Liquidity of Complex and Structured Derivatives*, SpringerBriefs in Finance, DOI 10.1007/978-3-319-45970-7_4

forecast/explain the future performance of the underlying. First, we want see how the SOD changes, if we shift the two main input parameters (the CDS spread or the applied volatility) by 25, 50 or even 100 basis points. Due to these observations, we hope to find the main driver for the SOD, i.e. whether the CDS spread or the implied volatility is the more sensible factor for the SOD's value. Further we aim to develop a time series analysis examining the SOD of 22 major German companies at several observation points in a time period of 33 months[1] and examine whether the SOD hypothesis holds. If the share price of a company reaches its SOD within the SOD's runtime, we expect the company to default. Otherwise we have to find explanations why the company did not default. At last, we set up linear regressions to observe the influence of the SOD on the underlying's performance. We use the SOD as the independent or explaining variable and the performance as the depending or explained variable. For SODs, we refer to our standard time periods of six months, one year and two years. Concerning the performance we calculate the ex post performance for the runtimes of six months, one year, and two years as well as the performance until the maturity of the SOD (the same maturity as the implied CDS). In an expansion of these linear regressions we implement a regulation indicator. This indicator is equal to one if the company is regulated and null otherwise. With this indicator we want to consider the theory of economic regulation by Stigler (1971) and by Peltzman (1976) stating that the "state protects the public" through regulation (here saving companies from bankruptcy).

There exist two ways to evaluate CDS contracts—the structural and the reduced form approach. The reduced form models described in O'Kane and Turnbull (2003) use only exogenously data (market data) to derive the default probabilities. This approach is very dynamic and purely based on market data, which are the reasons why we apply this method. The reduced form approach is very often used in practice whereas most research literature applies the structural method. The structural approach has its origin in Merton (1974) and Black and Scholes (1973). The major determinants of the probability of default are assumed to be the financial leverage, the volatility and the risk free rate. There have been many further developments in the structural model such as Longstaff and Schwartz (1995), who discovered a negative correlation between the CDS premia and the risk free rate, Leland and Toft (1996) and many more. Earlier research used the credit spread derived from corporate bond yield spreads minus the risk free rate, but Blanco et al. (2005) demonstrated that the CDS spreads represent the credit spread in a more reliable way. Since the financial crisis of 2007 and the following years it is very hard to define and construct a risk free rate. For more detail information on the impact of the financial crisis on the risk free rates and possible solutions look at Bianchetti (2010) and Pallavicini (2010). Many papers point out the linkage between equity volatilities and the credit default spread—to name a few Collin-Dufresne et al. (2001), Longstaff et al. (2005), Zhang et al. (2009). With their new implementation and estimation method for the structural model, Hull et al. (2004)

[1]The data set lasts from 2013-03-21 to 2015-12-22.

proved that the changes in the stock price and in the CDS spreads are locally perfect correlated. Zhang et al. (2009) used stochastic volatilities and jumps to show these variables can explain up to 69 % of the credit spread movement. The explanatory power by Ericsson et al. (2009) were only 60 %, but they used financial leverage, risk-free rate and equity volatilities as their determined variables. Carr and Wu (2009) showed a framework between stock options and credit default swaps. They conclude that deep out-of-the-money (DOOM) American put options prices are mainly driven by the probability of default and are more sensitive the longer the maturity of the option is. Cao et al. (2010) proved that implied volatilities are more suitable to predict the credit spread than historical volatilities.

In the past there have also been some publications about the CDS valuation with option-implied volatilities. Cao et al. (2011) used a modification of the structural approach to price a CDS and they found out that implied volatilities are more robust than historical volatilities for the CDS evaluation. Carr and Wu (2011) developed a robust link between DOOM American put options and so-called unit recovery claims (URC). A URC is a contract where the protection buyer receives one dollar if, and only if, the reference entity defaults before or at maturity. They introduced a default corridor $[A, B]$, within this interval the stock price can never reside. The stock price is either above the barrier B or, if it falls below B, a default is automatically triggered and the stock price jumps underneath the barrier of A. Further they proved that, if this corridor exists, a vertical spread of American put options scaled by the difference in strikes has the same payoff as a URC. Based on Carr and Wu (2011), Angelopoulos et al. (2012) revealed that large cross-market deviations in option prices and in CDS spread of the same entity enclose valid information on the future stock price.

This chapter is structured as follows.[2] In the Sects. 4.1 and 4.2 we describe the main topics of this chapter, first by explaining our methodology concerning the sensitivity and later by exploring the linear regression to analyse the predictability of the company's performance due to the SOD. The Sect. 4.3 deals with our data set, followed by the results of our research in Sect. 4.4. The last Sect. 4.5 concludes our research findings in a comprehensive way.

4.1 Sensitivity

One focus of this paper is to look at the sensitivity of the SOD due to changes in the main two market input parameters. At each of our nine observation dates, we changed the CDS market spreads as well as the volatility surface by 25, 50 and 100 basis points and determined the corresponding new SOD. The purpose of this study

[2]In our original paper, we review after the introduction the concept and deviation of the SOD. It is basically a brief version of the paper "Credit Default Swap from an equity option view", which we find in Sect. 3.1. Therefore, we do repeat this subchapter in this dissertation again.

is to observe how the strike of default reacts to a change in either one of the main parameters. We examine the sensitivity in two different ways. First, we just compare the absolute difference in the SOD, which is a rather intuitive way to look at it, and secondly, we calculate the deviation via the discrete approach

$$sensitivity = \frac{\Delta SOD}{\Delta parameter}.$$

A strong correlation between the SOD and the applied volatility has already been observed in our previous paper, but we have not yet calculated a discrete derivative towards the volatility.

When it comes to the sensitivity with respect to the CDS market spread, we have to distinguish two kinds of CDS market spread shifts. First, we simply shift the CDS market spread upwards by 25, 50 and 100 basis points and determine the shifted SOD. A shift downwards could lead to negative CDS spreads, which are not possible, and we want to test the sensitivity towards distress i.e. raising the CDS spread. The shift to a higher CDS market spread implies, because we assume a flat constant hazard rate structure, that the hazard rate increases, i.e. the probability of default increases. The probability of default until time t is determined via the constant hazard rate in the following way

$$P(t) = 1 - \mathrm{SR}(\mathrm{t}) = 1 - \exp(-\lambda \mathrm{t})$$

where λ is the constant hazard rate and $SR(t)$ is the survival probability until time t. Therefore the probability of default is higher if the hazard rate is higher. The calculation of the option price via the CDS premium leg is nothing more than discounted payments with an additional probability weight i.e. the CDS option price is equal to

$$\mathrm{p_{opt}(t)} := \mathrm{premium(t)} = \mathrm{s_c} * \frac{1}{2} \sum_{\mathrm{n=1}}^{\mathrm{N}} \Delta(\mathrm{t_n}, \mathrm{t_{n-1}}) * \mathrm{d_n} * (\mathrm{SR}(\mathrm{t_{n-1}}) - \mathrm{SR}(\mathrm{t_n}))$$

where N is the number of coupons until maturity, $\mathrm{t_n}$ is the time in years until the nth coupon, $\mathrm{d_n}$ is the discount factor until $\mathrm{t_n}$, the parameter $\mathrm{s_c}$ represents the contractual spread and $\Delta(\mathrm{t_n}, \mathrm{t_{n-1}})$ is the time difference between the nth and the $(n-1)$th coupon according to the agreed day count convention.[3] The $\mathrm{p_{opt}(t)}$ shows simply the premium leg of the CDS the option price, which we fit the American digital option against. This whole discussion leads us to the following result; if we just increase the CDS market spread we gain a higher hazard rate and a lower survival rate which leads to a minor CDS option price. On the one hand, the lower CDS option price implies a lower SOD with a higher probability of default. On the other hand, this is not the expected implication, since we would assume higher risk leads

[3]The standard day count convention for CDS contracts is ACT/360.

to a smaller risk cushion. In the market it is the standard procedure to raise the deal spread, if the CDS market spread moves above certain boundaries. This means, if we have a CDS market spread of 60 bps, it is most likely that on the next roll the deal spread rises from 25 to 50 bps an so one. All our observation points are placed on dates when new rolls are set up. Therefore, we did a second CDS sensitivity calculation. In such calculation we first change the CDS market spread and if this manipulated CDS market spread exceeded certain limits, then we also adjust the CDS deal spread. Due to the increase in deal spread the CDS option price raises as well as the SOD. We refer to such sensitivity calculations as adjusted shifts. For example, if a company has one-year CDS market spread of 42 bps and a deal spread of 50 bps. If we shift this market spread by 100 bps, then we also change the deal spread to 100 bps. Thus, from now on we always distinguish between the CDS shift and the CDS adjusted shift, where we also changed the deal spread if needed. In contrast to the CDS sensitivity, for the volatility sensitivity we simply shift the applied volatility by 25, 50 or 100 bps upwards.

4.2 Time Series Analysis

The second part of this paper deals with a time series analysis of the SOD. We take a look at historical SODs and if they have ever been reached. If in certain cases a company did fall below the SOD barrier without going bankrupt, we discuss the reasons for such scenario.

Additionally we study whether the SOD has an influence on the performance of the underlying. We derive the six month, one-year and two-year performances as well as the performance until the maturity of the CDS contract.[4] Then we will use a linear regression to measure the influence of the SOD to the yield performance of the company. Thus we simply want to examine the following linear regression

$$performance_i = \alpha_{i,j} + \beta_{i,j} * SOD_j + \epsilon_{i,j},$$

where i and j are the different tenors for the performance and the SOD, $\alpha_{i,j}$ is the interception of the regression and $\beta_{i,j}$ is the regression coefficient. Further we assume that the so-called error terms $\epsilon_{i,j}$ have an expected value zero, are uncorrelated and obtain the same variance σ^2 i.e.

$$Cov\left(\epsilon_{i,j}, \epsilon_{k,l}\right) = \left\{ \begin{matrix} \sigma^2 \; if \, j = k \, \text{and} \, j = l \\ 0 \end{matrix} \right\}.$$

[4]That means nine months for the six months contract, 15 months for the one-year contract and 27 months for the two-year contract.

For the performance we will consider the tenors mentioned above, whereas for the SOD we still have our three basic tenors (six months, one year-and two-year).

The theory of regulation by Stigler (1971) and Peltzman (1976) assumes that any government will support the survival of some industries in case of an upcoming bankruptcy. Example for such industries are energy, banks i.e. industries a national economy inevitable needs to keep on running. Thus we will expand the regression with the information, if the company is part of a regulated industry, as an additional explaining variable i.e.

$$performance_i = \alpha_{i,j} + \beta_{i,j} * SOD_j + \gamma_{i,j} * 1_{\{regulated\}} + \epsilon_{i,j},$$

where

$$1_{\{regulated\}} = \left\{ \begin{matrix} 1 & \textit{if}\ \text{the company is regulated} \\ 0 & \text{otherwise} \end{matrix} \right\}.$$

In some noticeable cases we want to test the regression on homoscedasticity i.e. whether the assumption on the constant variance for the error terms $\epsilon_{i,j}$ holds. For the test of homoscedasticity we will apply the Breusch-Pagan test where the null hypothesis is that the variance is constant (homoscedasticity). If the hypothesis is rejected, than the collection of random variable are heteroscedastic and in this case the significance of this regression is weakening since one of the assumptions is not valid any more.

A higher SOD implies that the markets believe that the default of the company occurs earlier than for a company with a lower SOD. Thus we would expect the parameters for the SOD to be negative meaning a higher SOD implies in general a worse performance. Further, we assume that the explanatory power of the SOD to the performance depends strongly on their tenor meaning the closer both tenors are, they better the R^2. For example the SOD for the six months CDS contract should have a higher R^2 (and thus explanatory power) for the six months performance than for the two-years performance and so on. At last we suggest that the additional variable of the regulated companies will increase the R^2.

4.3 Data Set

We looked at twenty-two German stock-listed companies, which are highly liquid and mostly members of the DAX either the MDAX. These entities are Allianz, BASF, BMW, Commerzbank, Continental, Deutsche Bank, Daimler, Deutsche Post, Deutsche Telekom, E.ON, HeidelbergCement, Henkel, Hannover Re, Linde, Metro, Munich RE, Porsche, RWE, Siemens, ThyssenKrupp, TUI and Volkswagen. We gathered the CDS data for each underlying market spreads with maturities of six months, one and two years. Furthermore, we gained the underlying's implied volatility surfaces from iVolatility[5] with maturities shorter than three years. The grid of the volatilities ranges from a moneyness of 0.4 up to 1 for each maturity. As described in Schmidt (2014b) we use a cubic spline extrapolation for strikes with moneyness below 0.4. We evaluated each company with three different maturities in each quarter starting 2011-03-21 and ending on 2013-03-20. Furthermore, we used different approaches for the sensitivity analysis and the time series analysis. For the calculation of the performances we gathered the EOD quotes from all companies beginning at the 2011-03-21 and ending at the 2015-12-22. Thus we were not able to derive the two-years performance for the last evaluation date (2013-03-20) and the performance until maturity of the two-year SODs on the last two evaluation dates (2013-03-20 and 2012-12-20). It is worth mentioning that the CDS contracts have fixed coupon dates (the 20th of each March, June, September and December) and that they are rolled each quarter. Therefore, the maturity date of the contracts is never reached (constant maturity). The time to maturity in years is at least as high as the maturity e.g. a six-month CDS in January matures in September of the same year and has a time to maturity higher than 0.5 years.

4.4 Results

Let us first take a look at the sensitivities. First we consider the non-adjusted CDS shift i.e. we shift the CDS market spread upwards by 25, 50 or 100 bps but the CDS deal spread remains unchanged. Then the derived constant hazard rate is higher than hazard rate of the non-shifted CDS market spread. This higher hazard rate leads to a lower CDS price and, therefore, the SOD of the non-adjusted CDS shift is assumed to be lower than the usual SOD. The results confirm these thoughts as Table 4.1 shows in a gross overview. Tables 4.2, 4.3, 4.4, 4.5, 4.6 and 4.7 present the results in detail. In both cases, the shifted CDS is lower than the non-shifted SOD. We observe the absolute difference to growth with either a prolongation of the maturity or increase in the basis point shift, i.e. a slightly lower SOD but with a higher probability of being reached. On average, the 25 basis points in the CDS shift decreased the SOD by about 0.19 basis points[6] for contracts with a maturity of six months and 2.95 basis points (bps) for contracts with a the two-year maturity.

Similar to the 100 bps shift in the CDS spread, the SOD reduces by 2.32 bps on average in the six months contract and 9.99 bps on average in the two-year contract. The deviation of the SOD with regard to CDS shift reflects more or less the same tendency. As the maturity increases so does the deviation of the sensitivity, but it keeps relatively constant over the size of the CDS market spread shift. If, on the other hand, we also shift the CDS deal spread, i.e. increase the CDS option price

[5]For further information visit www.ivolatility.com.

[6]In terms of moneyness it is 0.000019 smaller than the original SOD.

Table 4.1 Overview of all sensitivities on average, where each value is calculated based on 594 observations

Overview	CDS shift			CDS shift adjusted			Volatility shift		
	25	50	100	25	50	100	25	50	100
6 months (abs.)	−0.19	−0.97	−2.32	107.12	249.78	488.78	−23.61	−47.32	−94.00
1 year (abs.)	−2.21	−3.36	−5.14	126.97	245.86	447.59	−25.37	−49.00	−97.28
2 years (abs.)	−2.95	−4.90	−9.99	128.32	254.16	390.81	−24.91	−49.18	−98.10
6 months (dev.)	−0.01	−0.02	−0.02	4.28	5.00	4.89	−0.94	−0.95	−0.94
1 year (dev.)	−0.09	−0.07	−0.05	5.08	4.92	4.48	−1.01	−0.98	−0.97
2 years (dev.)	−0.12	−0.10	−0.10	5.13	5.08	3.91	−1.00	−0.98	−0.98

due to the higher coupon, we calculate a higher SOD. We notice for the adjusted shift, that not only the influence differs on the movement direction (positive sign), but also the size and its behaviour with respect to the maturity. The 25 bps adjusted shift influenced the SOD in our data set by about 107.12 bps in the six months contract and by up to 128.32 bps in the two-year contract. We find similar constant results for the 50 bps adjusted shift (from 245.89 to 254.16). The 100 bps shift shows extraordinary results because it has by far the biggest influence on the six months contracts. Such influence decreases over time from 488.78 for the one-year contracts to 390.81 for the two-year contracts. If we discuss the deviations it is roughly the same with the shifts, i.e. we can roughly say that if the market spread changes by one basis point with a respective change in the deal spread, then the SOD increases by about 4.75 bps. That equals 0.000475 in terms of moneyness. For the shift[7] in the volatility surface we evaluate based on higher volatilities, a raised the option price and an unchanged CDS price. As a result there should be a drop in the SOD value. This consideration is also proven by our data. Similar to the adjusted CDS, shift the volatility shift is more or less constant over the time, but the SOD decreases with an increase in the shift. A shift of 25 or even 100 bps in the volatility is not as big an influence as it is on the CDS spread due to their nature. Only if we take into regard the deviation again, the influence is pretty constant on the SOD. It is safe to say that a drift of one basis point in the volatility leads to a change in the SOD by one basis point, i.e. 0.0001 in-the-moneyness/SOD. These results are all not very surprising. However, it is worth to notice, that the time until

[7]We add 25, 50 or 100 bps to the applied volatility.

Table 4.2 This table displays the mean of the SOD and its absolute shifts with a maturity of six months, all values are based on the nine observation dates and the unit is as usual moneyness

6 month maturity	SOD	CDS shift			CDS shift adjusted			Volatility shift		
		25	50	100	25	50	100	25	50	100
Allianz	0.337443	0.337443	0.337443	0.337126	0.346718	0.353912	0.377962	0.335146	0.332559	0.327533
BASF	0.285551	0.285445	0.285445	0.285269	0.294367	0.31438	0.355992	0.282924	0.280521	0.275888
BMW	0.286274	0.286274	0.286133	0.285957	0.300274	0.314274	0.338642	0.284229	0.281919	0.277793
Commerzbank	0.195185	0.195185	0.195185	0.195079	0.199099	0.209009	0.212994	0.193933	0.192611	0.18956
Continental	0.296042	0.296042	0.29576	0.295478	0.315967	0.319916	0.328662	0.293397	0.290858	0.286732
Deutsche Bank	0.214703	0.214597	0.214597	0.214527	0.224472	0.231825	0.255065	0.212914	0.211332	0.207982
Daimler	0.279291	0.279291	0.279186	0.279186	0.296289	0.303624	0.329579	0.277211	0.27513	0.270753
Deutsche Post	0.334234	0.334234	0.334234	0.334128	0.348551	0.3683	0.40159	0.331765	0.328838	0.323742
Deutsche Telekom	0.388083	0.388083	0.387978	0.387978	0.397464	0.415872	0.443555	0.385368	0.382547	0.376587
E. ON	0.34462	0.344584	0.344584	0.344584	0.354917	0.375	0.404552	0.341877	0.339418	0.334551
HeidelbergCement	0.30038	0.30038	0.30038	0.300133	0.307997	0.322949	0.334763	0.298264	0.295901	0.291528
Henkel	0.363521	0.363521	0.363521	0.363521	0.369499	0.397217	0.432411	0.360753	0.358091	0.352215
Hannover Re	0.344514	0.344514	0.344408	0.344408	0.362534	0.380854	0.402118	0.34171	0.339083	0.33393
Linde	0.369816	0.369816	0.369816	0.369781	0.382088	0.402224	0.439005	0.366607	0.363433	0.357473
Metro	0.363539	0.363433	0.363186	0.363186	0.385297	0.385297	0.410194	0.360753	0.358232	0.353559
Munich RE	0.369146	0.369111	0.368934	0.368864	0.372461	0.392632	0.420033	0.366537	0.363997	0.358849
Porsche	0.324536	0.324536	0.324254	0.324078	0.328168	0.334622	0.360365	0.321927	0.319705	0.315222
RWE	0.347714	0.347714	0.347608	0.347396	0.3645	0.375247	0.404658	0.345448	0.342909	0.337972
Siemens	0.341357	0.34134	0.34134	0.341269	0.344161	0.369922	0.404763	0.338847	0.336341	0.331146
ThyssenKrupp	0.296959	0.296959	0.296959	0.296571	0.305987	0.32503	0.331765	0.294878	0.292586	0.287887
TUI	0.230379	0.230379	0.230203	0.22985	0.234153	0.242546	0.245649	0.228722	0.227452	0.223961
Volkswagen	0.293344	0.293344	0.293344	0.293159	0.307345	0.321503	0.347635	0.291493	0.28906	0.284978
Mean	0.313938	0.313919	0.313841	0.313706	0.32465	0.338916	0.362816	0.311577	0.309206	0.304538

Table 4.3 This table displays the mean of the SOD and its absolute shifts with a maturity of one year, all values are based on the nine observation dates and the unit is as usual moneyness

1 year maturity	SOD	CDS shift			CDS shift adjusted			Volatility shift		
		25	50	100	25	50	100	25	50	100
Allianz	0.322209	0.322103	0.321539	0.321539	0.326123	0.333388	0.355322	0.319705	0.317025	0.311841
BASF	0.260249	0.259931	0.259825	0.259473	0.267301	0.296289	0.325841	0.257427	0.255241	0.250551
BMW	0.238631	0.238067	0.238067	0.237961	0.248858	0.260319	0.287156	0.236021	0.23387	0.22978
Commerzbank	0.182648	0.182648	0.182296	0.181696	0.182648	0.189261	0.192505	0.181176	0.179316	0.176759
Continental	0.254465	0.254253	0.254112	0.253901	0.265855	0.270052	0.27908	0.252596	0.250304	0.245966
Deutsche Bank	0.179598	0.179351	0.178999	0.178858	0.190671	0.202308	0.220047	0.177447	0.175825	0.172757
Daimler	0.239478	0.239301	0.239301	0.239266	0.254042	0.257604	0.285075	0.237679	0.235457	0.231049
Deutsche Post	0.311242	0.311065	0.310959	0.310748	0.319458	0.340723	0.368159	0.308209	0.305458	0.299639
Deutsche Telekom	0.368088	0.368088	0.367912	0.367736	0.390058	0.39429	0.426063	0.365091	0.361529	0.355111
E. ON	0.317836	0.317166	0.317166	0.31706	0.344672	0.34841	0.37962	0.314697	0.311911	0.306304
HeidelbergCement	0.253689	0.253372	0.253337	0.25309	0.286944	0.295725	0.295513	0.25115	0.249352	0.245155
Henkel	0.3117	0.311594	0.311594	0.311523	0.324043	0.349327	0.377292	0.308984	0.306269	0.300486
Hannover Re	0.28712	0.286838	0.286838	0.286662	0.313639	0.322244	0.333282	0.28444	0.282148	0.277035
Linde	0.329861	0.329755	0.329755	0.329649	0.339841	0.358073	0.394783	0.326511	0.323937	0.317095
Metro	0.321609	0.321609	0.321609	0.321433	0.339912	0.339912	0.364844	0.318859	0.316496	0.310571
Munich RE	0.329332	0.328944	0.328909	0.328556	0.33635	0.361917	0.382088	0.326511	0.32369	0.318365
Porsche	0.269805	0.269523	0.269523	0.269417	0.273191	0.293186	0.306093	0.267337	0.265327	0.261095
RWE	0.314979	0.314556	0.314451	0.314274	0.337373	0.345695	0.372179	0.312158	0.309372	0.304012
Siemens	0.314592	0.314592	0.314592	0.314556	0.324607	0.344884	0.375141	0.31177	0.309161	0.303342
ThyssenKrupp	0.254536	0.254324	0.254324	0.253936	0.264727	0.278092	0.277775	0.25242	0.250022	0.24579
TUI	0.210102	0.210067	0.209679	0.209679	0.210067	0.209679	0.209679	0.208092	0.206434	0.203507
Volkswagen	0.237924	0.237677	0.2375	0.237359	0.248644	0.25919	0.286838	0.235598	0.233747	0.229462
Mean	0.277713	0.277492	0.277377	0.277199	0.29041	0.302299	0.322472	0.275176	0.272813	0.267985

Table 4.4 This table displays the mean of the SOD and its absolute shifts with a maturity of two years, all values are based on the nine observation dates and the unit is as usual moneyness

2 years maturity	SOD	CDS shift			CDS shift adjusted			Volatility shift		
		25	50	100	25	50	100	25	50	100
Allianz	0.254782	0.254253	0.254077	0.253689	0.258344	0.282254	0.287261	0.251609	0.24907	0.243886
BASF	0.227276	0.226923	0.226817	0.226324	0.239301	0.252067	0.281513	0.224349	0.22188	0.217084
BMW	0.189649	0.189225	0.18919	0.188767	0.197724	0.210278	0.224278	0.18725	0.18517	0.18115
Commerzbank	0.149658	0.149517	0.149376	0.148671	0.153996	0.157628	0.166444	0.147895	0.146555	0.143205
Continental	0.200369	0.200087	0.199946	0.199382	0.225477	0.225195	0.224666	0.198324	0.195926	0.191659
Deutsche Bank	0.143945	0.143945	0.143452	0.143205	0.154278	0.167361	0.171381	0.142535	0.14056	0.137421
Daimler	0.195538	0.195397	0.195185	0.194903	0.199382	0.221387	0.225795	0.193563	0.191447	0.187286
Deutsche Post	0.242299	0.242087	0.241876	0.241241	0.267654	0.282148	0.306833	0.239513	0.236515	0.230273
Deutsche Telekom	0.36107	0.360506	0.36033	0.359695	0.365126	0.389494	0.398804	0.357473	0.353947	0.347211
E. ON	0.291528	0.291176	0.29114	0.290506	0.291176	0.300485	0.326476	0.288566	0.285816	0.279609
HeidelbergCement	0.202026	0.201603	0.20125	0.200686	0.216591	0.216344	0.228722	0.199699	0.197654	0.19381
Henkel	0.249387	0.249069	0.248682	0.248294	0.274143	0.2831	0.312687	0.246601	0.243533	0.237961
Hannover Re	0.218918	0.218742	0.218565	0.218001	0.223538	0.235281	0.238843	0.216979	0.21444	0.20982
Linde	0.269558	0.269241	0.269135	0.268712	0.290224	0.3044	0.33501	0.266631	0.263493	0.257498
Metro	0.274249	0.274178	0.273931	0.273296	0.297523	0.297312	0.306657	0.271709	0.268994	0.263246
Munich RE	0.262964	0.262576	0.262188	0.2618	0.275342	0.299745	0.314733	0.260037	0.257039	0.251891
Porsche	0.190742	0.19053	0.190283	0.190001	0.201638	0.210737	0.224067	0.189049	0.186792	0.182807
RWE	0.318047	0.317554	0.317518	0.316848	0.322209	0.341005	0.349927	0.314733	0.311947	0.304964
Siemens	0.260742	0.26046	0.26046	0.260002	0.286203	0.290647	0.320093	0.257639	0.25517	0.248893
ThyssenKrupp	0.222127	0.221669	0.221669	0.220964	0.238279	0.270722	0.269206	0.219765	0.217719	0.212853
TUI	0.150575	0.15054	0.150293	0.149693	0.172086	0.17184	0.188767	0.148953	0.147754	0.145109
Volkswagen	0.176742	0.176424	0.176036	0.175542	0.184253	0.201921	0.20982	0.17452	0.17258	0.168736
Mean	0.229645	0.22935	0.229155	0.228646	0.242477	0.255061	0.268726	0.227154	0.224727	0.219835

Table 4.5 This table displays the mean of the derivations of the SOD shifts with a maturity of six months, all values are based on the nine observation dates and the unit is as usual moneyness

6 months maturity	CDS shift			CDS shift adjusted			Volatility shift		
	25	50	100	25	50	100	25	50	100
Allianz	0	0	−0.000003	0.000371	0.000329	0.000405	−0.000092	−0.000098	−0.000099
BASF	−0.000004	−0.000002	−0.000003	0.000353	0.000577	0.000704	−0.000105	−0.000101	−0.000097
BMW	0	−0.000003	−0.000003	0.00056	0.00056	0.000523	−0.000082	−0.000087	−0.000085
Commerzbank	0	0	−0.000001	0.000157	0.000276	0.000178	−0.00005	−0.000052	−0.000056
Continental	0	−0.000006	−0.000006	0.000797	0.000478	0.000326	−0.000106	−0.000104	−0.000093
Deutsche Bank	−0.000004	−0.000002	−0.000002	0.000391	0.000342	0.000404	−0.000072	−0.000067	−0.000067
Daimler	0	−0.000002	−0.000001	0.00068	0.000487	0.000503	−0.000083	−0.000083	−0.000085
Deutsche Post	0	0	−0.000001	0.000573	0.000682	0.000674	−0.000099	−0.000108	−0.000105
Deutsche Telekom	0	−0.000002	−0.000001	0.000375	0.000556	0.000555	−0.000109	−0.000111	−0.000115
E. ON	−0.000001	−0.000001	0	0.000412	0.000608	0.000599	−0.00011	−0.000104	−0.000101
HeidelbergCement	0	0	−0.000003	0.000305	0.000451	0.000344	−0.000085	−0.00009	−0.000088
Henkel	0	0	0	0.000239	0.000674	0.000689	−0.000111	−0.000109	−0.000113
Hannover Re	0	−0.000002	−0.000001	0.000721	0.000727	0.000576	−0.000112	−0.000109	−0.000106
Linde	0	0	0	0.000491	0.000648	0.000692	−0.000129	−0.000128	−0.000123
Metro	−0.000004	−0.000007	−0.000004	0.00087	0.000435	0.000467	−0.000112	−0.000106	−0.0001
Munich RE	−0.000001	−0.000004	−0.000003	0.000133	0.00047	0.000509	−0.000105	−0.000103	−0.000103
Porsche	0	−0.000006	−0.000005	0.000145	0.000202	0.000358	−0.000105	−0.000097	−0.000093
RWE	0	−0.000002	−0.000003	0.000671	0.000551	0.000569	−0.000091	−0.000096	−0.000097
Siemens	−0.000001	0	−0.000001	0.000112	0.000571	0.000634	−0.000101	−0.0001	−0.000102
ThyssenKrupp	0	0	−0.000004	0.000361	0.000561	0.000348	−0.000083	−0.000088	−0.000091
TUI	0	−0.000004	−0.000005	0.000151	0.000243	0.000153	−0.000066	−0.000058	−0.000064
Volkswagen	0	0	−0.000002	0.00056	0.000563	0.000543	−0.000074	−0.000086	−0.000084
Mean	−0.000001	−0.000002	−0.000002	0.000429	0.0005	0.000489	−0.000095	−0.000095	−0.000094

Table 4.6 This table displays the mean of the derivations of the SOD shifts with a maturity of one year, all values are based on the nine observation dates and the unit is as usual moneyness

1 year maturity	CDS shift			CDS shift adjusted			Volatility shift		
	25	50	100	25	50	100	25	50	100
Allianz	−0.000004	−0.000013	−0.000007	0.000157	0.000224	0.000331	−0.0001	−0.000104	−0.000104
BASF	−0.000013	−0.000008	−0.000008	0.000282	0.000721	0.000656	−0.000113	−0.0001	−0.000097
BMW	−0.000022	−0.000011	−0.000007	0.000409	0.000434	0.000485	−0.000104	−0.000095	−0.000089
Commerzbank	0	−0.000007	−0.00001	0	0.000132	0.000098	−0.000059	−0.000067	−0.000059
Continental	−0.000008	−0.000007	−0.000006	0.000456	0.000312	0.000246	−0.000075	−0.000083	−0.000085
Deutsche Bank	−0.00001	−0.000012	−0.000008	0.000443	0.000454	0.000405	−0.000086	−0.000076	−0.000068
Daimler	−0.000007	−0.000004	−0.000002	0.000583	0.000362	0.000456	−0.000072	−0.000081	−0.000084
Deutsche Post	−0.000007	−0.000006	−0.000005	0.000329	0.00059	0.000569	−0.000121	−0.000116	−0.000116
Deutsche Telekom	0	−0.000004	−0.000004	0.000879	0.000524	0.00058	−0.00012	−0.000131	−0.00013
E. ON	−0.000027	−0.000013	−0.000008	0.001073	0.000612	0.000618	−0.000126	−0.000119	−0.000115
HeidelbergCement	−0.000013	−0.000007	−0.000006	0.00133	0.000841	0.000418	−0.000102	−0.000087	−0.000085
Henkel	−0.000004	−0.000002	−0.000002	0.000494	0.000753	0.000656	−0.000109	−0.000109	−0.000112
Hannover Re	−0.000011	−0.000006	−0.000005	0.001061	0.000703	0.000462	−0.000107	−0.000099	−0.000101
Linde	−0.000004	−0.000002	−0.000002	0.000399	0.000564	0.000649	−0.000134	−0.000119	−0.000128
Metro	0	0	−0.000002	0.000732	0.000366	0.000432	−0.00011	−0.000102	−0.00011
Munich RE	−0.000015	−0.000008	−0.000008	0.000281	0.000652	0.000528	−0.000113	−0.000113	−0.00011
Porsche	−0.000011	−0.000006	−0.000004	0.000135	0.000468	0.000363	−0.000099	−0.00009	−0.000087
RWE	−0.000017	−0.000011	−0.000007	0.000896	0.000614	0.000572	−0.000113	−0.000112	−0.000109
Siemens	0	0	0	0.000401	0.000606	0.000605	−0.000113	−0.000109	−0.000113
ThyssenKrupp	−0.000008	−0.000004	−0.000006	0.000408	0.000471	0.000232	−0.000085	−0.00009	−0.000087
TUI	−0.000001	−0.000008	−0.000004	−0.000001	−0.000008	−0.000004	−0.00008	−0.000073	−0.000066
Volkswagen	−0.00001	−0.000008	−0.000006	0.000429	0.000425	0.000489	−0.000093	−0.000084	−0.000084
Mean	−0.000009	−0.000007	−0.000005	0.000508	0.000492	0.000448	−0.000102	−0.000098	−0.000097

Table 4.7 This table displays the mean of the derivations of the SOD shifts with a maturity of two years, all values are based on the nine observation dates and the unit is as usual moneyness

2 years maturity	CDS shift			CDS shift adjusted			Volatility shift		
	25	50	100	25	50	100	25	50	100
Allianz	−0.000021	−0.000014	−0.000011	0.000143	0.000549	0.000325	−0.000127	−0.000114	−0.000109
BASF	−0.000014	−0.000009	−0.00001	0.000481	0.000496	0.000542	−0.000117	−0.000108	−0.000102
BMW	−0.000017	−0.000009	−0.000009	0.000323	0.000412	0.000346	−0.000096	−0.00009	−0.000085
Commerzbank	−0.000006	−0.000006	−0.00001	0.000173	0.000159	0.000168	−0.000071	−0.000062	−0.000065
Continental	−0.000011	−0.000008	−0.00001	0.001004	0.000497	0.000243	−0.000082	−0.000089	−0.000087
Deutsche Bank	0	−0.00001	−0.000008	0.000413	0.000468	0.000274	−0.000057	−0.000068	−0.000065
Daimler	−0.000006	−0.000007	−0.000006	0.000154	0.000517	0.000303	−0.000079	−0.000082	−0.000083
Deutsche Post	−0.000008	−0.000008	−0.000011	0.001014	0.000797	0.000645	−0.000112	−0.000116	−0.00012
Deutsche Telekom	−0.000023	−0.000015	−0.000014	0.000162	0.000569	0.000378	−0.000144	−0.000142	−0.000139
E. ON	−0.000014	−0.000008	−0.00001	−0.000014	0.000179	0.00035	−0.000119	−0.000114	−0.000119
HeidelbergCement	−0.000017	−0.000015	−0.000014	0.000583	0.000286	0.000267	−0.000093	−0.000087	−0.000082
Henkel	−0.000013	−0.000014	−0.000011	0.00099	0.000674	0.000633	−0.000112	−0.000117	−0.000114
Hannover Re	−0.000007	−0.000007	−0.000009	0.000185	0.000327	0.000199	−0.000078	−0.00009	−0.000091
Linde	−0.000013	−0.000008	−0.000009	0.000827	0.000697	0.000655	−0.000117	−0.000122	−0.00012
Metro	−0.000003	−0.000006	−0.00001	0.000931	0.000461	0.000324	−0.000102	−0.000105	−0.00011
Munich RE	−0.000015	−0.000015	−0.000012	0.000495	0.000736	0.000518	−0.000117	−0.000119	−0.000111
Porsche	−0.000008	−0.000009	−0.000008	0.000436	0.0004	0.000333	−0.000068	−0.000079	−0.000079
RWE	−0.00002	−0.000011	−0.000012	0.000167	0.000459	0.000319	−0.000133	−0.000122	−0.000131
Siemens	−0.000011	−0.000006	−0.000008	0.001018	0.000598	0.000594	−0.000124	−0.000112	−0.000118
ThyssenKrupp	−0.000018	−0.000009	−0.000012	0.000646	0.000972	0.000471	−0.000095	−0.000088	−0.000093
TUI	−0.000001	−0.000006	−0.000009	0.00086	0.000425	0.000382	−0.000065	−0.000056	−0.000055
Volkswagen	−0.000013	−0.000014	−0.000012	0.0003	0.000504	0.000331	−0.000089	−0.000083	−0.00008
Mean	−0.000012	−0.00001	−0.00001	0.000513	0.000508	0.000391	−0.0001	−0.000098	−0.000098

Fig. 4.1 The share price of Commerzbank with the 6 months SOD (*red line*), the 12 months SOD (*green line*) and the 24 months SOD (*purple line*). We observe that according to the SOD theory that after the SOD values have been hit, the company should have defaulted

maturity and the size of the shift does not essentially influence the change in the SOD per basis point for the adjusted CDS shift and minor volatility shifts.[8]

Now we will examine the time series analysis, i.e. if there have been any theoretical defaults according to our theory (of the SOD). The data show, that two of the companies should have gone bankrupt. First, Commerzbank hit the SOD Barrier and thus should have defaulted in all maturities starting on 2011-03-21, as we see in Fig. 4.1, and in the two-year maturity starting on 2011-06-20. Yet, why did the bank not collapse? From our point of view, there are two main reasons. First, the "Einlagensicherungsfonds" (deposit guarantee fund) of the Bundesverband Deutscher Banken (Federal Association of German Banks) covers any losses of all non-banking account to a bankruptcy up to €100,000. Non-banking accounts include all individual deposits, private companies and minor corporations. Furthermore, on 2009-01-08 the German government became shareholder of Commerzbank by buying 25 % plus one share to avoid possible fallout of the bank. Therefore, Commerzbank's survival despite hitting the SOD can be explained.

The second company meeting the SOD is RWE AG. The 6 month SOD starting on 2011-03-21 should have been hit on 2011-09-12 as you can see at Fig. 4.2. Since RWE is a utility company, the share/company was heavily affected by the nuclear disaster of Fukushima in the aftermath of 2011-03-11. In the year 2000, the former cabinet formed by Social Democrats and the Green Party decided to opt out of nuclear energy all together, meaning all nuclear power plants had to be closed 32 years after their initial operation. In 2009, the newly elected government formed by Christian Democrats and the FDP (liberal party) decided to extend the in-service time of nuclear power plants by eight to twelve years, depending on the respective year of construction. Due to such prolongation, utility companies again started to

[8]In terms of volatilities shifts up to 100 bps can be labelled as a minor shift since the average used volatilities is about 43.7 %.

Fig. 4.2 The share price of RWE with the 6 month SOD (*red line*), the 12 month SOD (*green line*) and the 24 month SOD (*purple line*). We observe that, according to the SOD theory, after the SOD value has been reached, the company should have defaulted

invest in the nuclear power plants, which are a cheap way to produce energy. Due to the nuclear catastrophe in Japan, however, the conservative-liberal government changed its mind and pronounced the retreatment of the prolongation in June 2011. As a consequence, all nuclear power plants have to be shut down in 2022 at the latest. RWE and other utility companies directly (in April 2011) accused the government that it is not their right to shut down all the plants at once. They have sued the government to pay several Billion euros. That trial is still being pending and expected to have a reasonable chance of a considerable compensation payment. The perspective of a payment of such dimension can explain the non-bankruptcy or non-default of RWE. At last it is worth to mention that both companies are regulated companies according to the theory of economic regulation [by Sitgler (1971) and its more general theory by Peltzman (1976)]. Thus the government helps these companies to survive in order to the "protection of the public".

Now we discuss the results for the performance analysis according to the maturity of the SOD. We start with the six-month SOD, followed by the one-year SOD and completed with the two-year SOD. For each SOD maturity, we view the simpler regression and then we examine the regressions including the regulation indicator. For the verification on the significance of the linear regression model to the fitted data set we will look at the F-test and in order to check the significance of the single parameters we will interrogate the p-value. For both tests we set the confidence level at 5 %, i.e. if the values are above 0.05, the regression or the parameter is not significant. Before we go into detail on the actual results, we want to mention that the sample size with 176 for the two-years performance, 154 for the maturity performance of the 2 years SOD and otherwise with 198 observation points is large enough to discuss the statistical results.

The results for the simpler regression with respect to the six months SOD are listed in Table 4.8. First, we obtain that only the six months performance and the performance until maturity of the SOD are statically significant according to the

Table 4.8 The regression results (without the indicator for regulated companies) for the six month SOD, where the time until maturity is equal to nine months

Performance	6 Months	1 Year	2 Years	Maturity
n	198	198	176	198
R^2	0.0321	0.0079	0.0175	0.0243
Standard error	0.2213	0.2807	0.2866	0.2600
Significant F	0.0115	0.2124	0.0804	0.0284
Interception (coefficient)	0.1470	0.2191	0.2536	0.2243
Interception (std. error)	0.0482	0.0611	0.0679	0.0566
Interception (p-value)	0.0026	0.0004	0.0003	0.0001
SOD (coefficient)	−0.3704	−0.2303	−0.3829	−0.3766
SOD (std. error)	0.1452	0.1841	0.2177	0.1705
SOD (p-value)	0.0115	0.2124	0.0804	0.0284

F-value, i.e. the value is below 0.05. Thus only the shorter performance can be explained to some part with the six months SOD, which was one of the assumptions from Sect. 4.2. The R^2's are for all performances rather poorly and does not exceed 4 % for the statistical significant cases, i.e. the six months SOD does not really explain the company's performance. At last, we observe that the coefficient for the SOD is—as we expected—always negative, meaning that a higher SOD tends to cause a minor performance of the underlying and the absolute value of the SOD coefficient is larger for longer maturities. The standard errors for the regression as well as for each parameter also increase if the time period is extended for the performance.

We find the values of the regression with the consideration of the regulation indicator in Table 4.9. First, it is surprising that with the addition of the regulation

Table 4.9 The regression results including the indicator for regulated companies for the six month SOD, where the time until maturity is equal to nine months

Performance	6 Months	1 Year	2 Years	Maturity
n	198	198	176	198
R^2	0.0399	0.0359	0.0445	0.0453
Standard error	0.2210	0.2774	0.2834	0.2578
Significant F	0.0189	0.0284	0.0195	0.0109
Interception (coefficient)	0.1610	0.2523	0.2867	0.2511
Interception (std. error)	0.0494	0.0620	0.0688	0.0576
Interception (p-value)	0.0013	0.0001	0.0000	0.0000
SOD (coefficient)	−0.3626	−0.2118	−0.3617	−0.3616
SOD (std. error)	0.1451	0.1821	0.2155	0.1693
SOD (p-value)	0.0133	0.2464	0.0951	0.0339
Is_regulated (coefficient)	−0.0401	−0.0954	−0.0962	−0.0772
Is_regulated (std. error)	0.0320	0.0401	0.0435	0.0373
Is_regulated (p-value)	0.2111	0.0184	0.0282	0.0397

Table 4.10 The regression results (without the indicator for regulated companies) for the one-year SOD, where the time until maturity is equal to 15 months

Performance	6 Months	1 Year	2 Years	Maturity
n	198	198	176	198
R^2	0.0825	0.0352	0.0701	0.0484
Standard error	0.2155	0.2768	0.4462	0.3256
Significant F	0.0000	0.0081	0.0004	0.0018
Interception (coefficient)	0.2052	0.2897	0.6852	0.3934
Interception (std. error)	0.0443	0.0569	0.0998	0.0669
Interception (p-value)	0.0000	0.0000	0.0000	0.0000
SOD (coefficient)	−0.6282	−0.5144	−1.3032	−0.7142
SOD (std. error)	0.1497	0.1923	0.3600	0.2262
SOD (p-value)	0.0000	0.0081	0.0004	0.0018

indicator to the linear regression all performances are significant. As one might expect, the standard errors are higher for performances with longer time periods. Nevertheless, the p-value for the SOD coefficient for the one and two-year performances is not statistically significant, which implies that the regression are no longer of interest for us, because the SOD coefficient is the main independent variable in our analysis. The coefficient for the SOD and the regulation indicator are again negative and are decreasing with a longer maturity of the performance. The R^2's are still rather poorly for the statistical significant cases, but the values are, as we expected, higher than in the simpler regression.

The results for one-year SOD are listed in Tables 4.10 and 4.11. In the case of the simpler regression, the results are in Table 4.10 displayed, we notice that the regression is statistically significant for all performances according to the F-value.

Table 4.11 The regression results including the indicator for regulated companies for the one-year SOD, where the time until maturity is equal to 15 months

Performance	6 Months	1 Year	2 Years	Maturity
n	198	198	176	198
R^2	0.0869	0.0584	0.1184	0.0803
Standard error	0.2155	0.2742	0.4357	0.3209
Significant F	0.0001	0.0028	0.0000	0.0003
Interception (coefficient)	0.2135	0.3134	0.7383	0.4264
Interception (std. error)	0.0451	0.0574	0.0989	0.0672
Interception (p-value)	0.0000	0.0000	0.0000	0.0000
SOD (coefficient)	−0.6132	−0.4713	−1.1821	−0.6544
SOD (std. error)	0.1505	0.1914	0.3537	0.2241
SOD (p-value)	0.0001	0.0147	0.0010	0.0039
Is_regulated (coefficient)	−0.0304	−0.0874	−0.2070	−0.1212
Is_regulated (std. error)	0.0313	0.0398	0.0672	0.0466
Is_regulated (p-value)	0.3323	0.0295	0.0024	0.0101

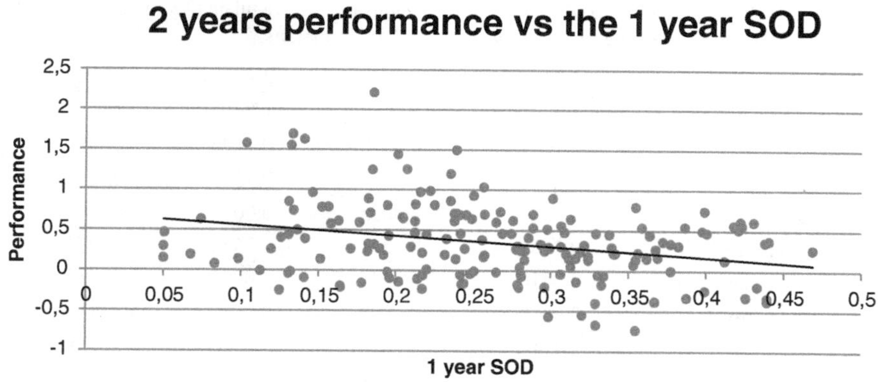

Fig. 4.3 The plot including the regression assumes that in case of the one-year SOD, the error terms seem to be heteroscedastic

For this set of linear regressions have the R^2's improved for all performances compared to the values from the simpler linear regression of the six months SOD. It is rather surprising that the R^2's for the six month and the two-year performances are higher than for the other performances, which have runtimes closer to the SOD. We presumed that it would be the other way around and we do not know any plausible reason for this occurrence. The coefficients for the SOD and the interception are always negative and are decreasing with the time period of the performances as we have seen before. Further, it is worth mentioning that the standard errors are always the highest for two-year performances. Because the range of a company's performance broadens with an increase in the time period, this phenomenon can be easily explained.

Additionally, we carried out a test of heteroscedasticity for the two-year performances with the one-year SOD as the independent variable. As Fig. 4.3 assumes the error terms tend to be heteroscedastic. Since a figure is not enough to support any assumption, we ran a Breusch-Pagan test on this regression, as noted in Sect. 4.2. The test showed that the homoscedasticity could be rejected with a confidence above 98 %. Therefore the good significance as detected above needs to be reduced. The test for heteroscedasticity for different performances showed the same conclusion.

The R^2's are again higher, if the regression is expanded by the regulation indicator as illustrated in Table 4.11 for the one-year SOD. As in the simpler regression, the R^2's for the six month and two-year performances is higher than for the other performances. The R^2 for the two-year performance exceeds 0.1, meaning that more than 10 % of the movements in the two-year performance can be explained by the one-year SOD and the regulation indicator. The standard errors on the other hand are again the highest for the two-year performances. In case of the six-month performance, the regulation indicator is not statistically significant. All other regressions and parameters are statistically significant. The coefficients for the

Table 4.12 The regression results (without the indicator for regulated companies) for the two-year SOD, where the time until maturity is equal to 27 months

Performance	6 Months	1 Year	2 Years	Maturity
n	198	198	176	154
R^2	0.1034	0.0596	0.1190	0.1508
Standard error	0.2130	0.2733	0.4343	0.4781
Significant F	0.0000	0.0005	0.0000	0.0000
Interception (coefficient)	0.2161	0.3231	0.7544	0.9127
Interception (std. error)	0.0418	0.0537	0.0906	0.1062
Interception (p-value)	0.0000	0.0000	0.0000	0.0000
SOD (coefficient)	−0.8070	−0.7678	−1.8535	−2.3525
SOD (std. error)	0.1698	0.2178	0.3824	0.4528
SOD (p-value)	0.0000	0.0005	0.0000	0.0000

SOD as well as for the regulation indicators are strictly negative but not strictly decreasing in this case.

Lastly, we consider the two-year SOD. As we gather from Table 4.12, all regressions as well as all parameters are statistically significant. The R^2's are highest for the longest runtime and even exceed 15 % for the performance until maturity, which in this case lasts 27 months. The coefficients for the SOD are strictly negative and are the lowest for the longest runtimes. With an increase in the length of the time period for the performance, the standard errors are again increasing.

For the performance until maturity with the two-year SOD as the explaining variable we visualize the data including the regression in Fig. 4.4. As one might assume, the regression seems to be heteroscedastic. The according Breusch-Pagan Test revealed a value of 0.0041 i.e. the homoscedasticity can be rejected with a

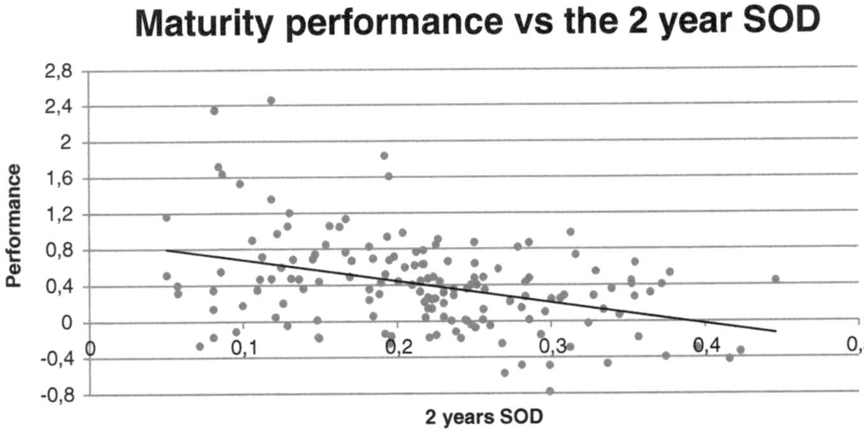

Fig. 4.4 The plot including the regression assumes that in case of the two-year SOD, the error terms appear to be heteroscedastic

Table 4.13 The regression results including the indicator for regulated companies for the two-year SOD, where the time until maturity is equal to 27 months

Performance	6 Months	1 Year	2 Years	Maturity
n	198	198	176	154
R^2	0.1048	0.0761	0.1515	0.1756
Standard error	0.2134	0.2716	0.4275	0.4726
Significant F	0.0000	0.0004	0.0000	0.0000
Interception (coefficient)	0.2191	0.3364	0.7797	0.9313
Interception (std. error)	0.0423	0.0538	0.0897	0.1054
Interception (p-value)	0.0000	0.0000	0.0000	0.0000
SOD (coefficient)	−0.7895	−0.6928	−1.6483	−2.1193
SOD (std. error)	0.1730	0.2201	0.3847	0.4608
SOD (p-value)	0.0000	0.0019	0.0000	0.0000
Is_regulated (coefficient)	−0.0174	−0.0744	−0.1726	−0.1701
Is_regulated (std. error)	0.0314	0.0399	0.0670	0.0797
Is_regulated (p-value)	0.5809	0.0637	0.0108	0.0345

confidence level of more than 99 %, which implies that the significance of the regression is weaken. We found similar results for various performances.

In the last set of regressions, displayed in Table 4.13, we observe that the R^2 s have again increased and exceed 17.5 %, which is a rather high value. All regressions are statistically significant, where the regulation indicator is not always statistically significant for the lower maturities. The coefficients for the SOD and the regulation indicator are again negative and have the lowest values for the longest time periods.

4.5 Conclusion

We are able to state that in terms of adjusted CDS shifts and volatility shift the sensitivity is linear in the direction of time to maturity. In other words there is no noteworthy difference in the SOD-change, if we apply a shift on a six months contract or a two-year contract. Further, we can establish that a CDS shift is only of importance, if it is accomplished with a shift in the deal spread. Otherwise its effect is negligible to the SOD. The deviation on the volatility is smaller than the deviation on the adjusted CDS spread which is a bit surprising at first, but the change on an e.g. 200 bps CDS spread by 100 bps is relatively larger than the change of the applied volatility of e.g. 35 % by 1 %.

The historical data of the 22 underlyings have shown that the SOD is a valid risk measure. The theoretical defaults can be explained with reason and in all other cases the SOD worked as promised. It is reasonable to argue that 22 underlyings on only nine evaluation dates is not sufficient enough to conclude that the SOD is stable enough but our work and examination of this figure give us a good confidence about the idea and construction of the SOD theory.

Overall, we observe that SOD can to some degree explain part the performance of the respective companies. The analysis has shown that a higher SOD generally implies a lower performance. Furthermore, the results suggest that the influence of the SOD on the performance is higher longer the runtimes of SOD and the performances are. The best R^2-values (between 11 and 18 %) were received for the two-year SOD. The additional information whether a company is regulated by the government usually strengthened this statement. Interestingly, the coefficient of the regulation indication is negative, meaning that regulated companies seem not to perform as well as unregulated firms. Both coefficient are the lowest (or absolutely the highest) for the longest performance time period, that means the longer the time period for the performance measurement is higher is the weight for the SOD value and the regulation indicator.

Future research topics could be to use stochastic volatilities and even jumps, which are very interesting for DOOM options in particular. The determination of the SOD could be improved by a different assumption of the recovery rate. A completely different idea is to compare the default risk of the CDS spread via the hazard rate and to derive the probability of default using the applied volatility with a binomial tree method. We derived a straightforward method to price American digital options with a binary tree model. Even if it sounds quiet easy it is not as easy as we assumed before and only found a recursive solution. Our paper did take a look at what we call the inverse optimal leverage, meaning the structure of debt and equity based on our threshold.

References

G. Angelopoulus, D. Giamouridis, G. Nikolakakis, Stock return predictability of cross-market deviations in option prices and credit default swap spreads. Available at SSRN 1991179 (2012)

M. Bianchetti, Two curves, one price: pricing & hedging interest rate derivatives decoupling forwarding and discounting yield curves. Risk Mag. **10**(8), 70–75 (2010)

F. Black, M.S. Scholes, The pricing of options and corporate liabilities. J. Polit. Econ. (7), 637–654 (1973)

R. Blanco, S. Brennan, I.W. Marsh, An empirical analysis of the dynamic relationship between investment-grade bonds and credit default swaps. J. Finance **60**(5), 2255–2281 (2005)

C. Cao, F. Yu, Z. Zhong, The information content of option-implied volatility for credit default swap valuation. J. Finan. Markets **13**(3), 321–343 (2010)

P. Carr, L. Wu, Stock options and credit default swaps: a joint framework for valuation and estimation. J. Finan. Econ. (2009): nbp010

P. Carr, L. Wu, A simple robust link between American puts and credit protection. Rev. Finan. Stud. **24**(2), 473–505 (2011)

P. Collin-Dufresne, R. Goldstein, J. Martin, The determination of credit spread changes. J. Finance **56**(6), 2177–2207 (2001)

J. Ericsson, K. Jacobs, R.A. Oviedo, The determinants of credit default swap premia. J. Finan. Quant. Anal. **44**(1), 109–132 (2009)

J.C. Hull, I. Nelken, A. White, Merton's model, credit risk, and volatility skews. J. Credit Risk **1** (1), 8–23 (2004)

H.E. Leland, K.B. Toft, Optimal capital structure, endogenous bankruptcy, and the term structure of credit spread. J. Finance **51**(3), 987–1019 (1996)

F.A. Longstaff, E.S. Schwartz, A simple approach to valuing risky fixed and floating rate debt. J. Finance **50**(3), 789–819 (1995)

F.A. Longstaff, S. Mithal, E. Neis, Corporate yield spreads: default risk or liquidity? New evidence from the credit-default swap market. J. Finance **60**(5), 2213–2253 (2005)

R.C. Merton, On the pricing of corporate debt: the risk structure of interest rates. J. Finance **29**(2), 449–479 (1974)

D. O'Kane, S. Turnbull, Valuation of credit default swaps. Lehman Brothers quantitative credit research quarterly (2003)

A. Pallavicini, M. Taremghi, Interest-rate modeling with multiple yield curves. Available at SSRN 1629688 (2010)

S. Peltzman, Toward a more general theory of regulation. J. Law Econ. 211–240 (1976)

M.F. Schmidt, Strike of default: sensitivity and time series analysis. Unpublished working paper (2014a)

M.F. Schmidt, Credit default swaps from an equity point of view. World Finance Conference (2014b)

G. Stigler, The theory of economic regulation. Bell J. Econ. Manage. Sci. 3–21 (1971)

B.Y. Zhang, H. Zhou, H. Zhu, Explaining credit default swap spreads with the equity volatility and jump risks of individual firms. Rev. Finan. Stud. **22**(12), 5099–5131 (2009)

Chapter 5
Conclusion

In the first paper of this dissertation, we dealt with the evaluation of CDS contracts. This dissertation empirically proves that the evaluation of CDS contracts is not as simple and straightforward as one might assume. Even if we slightly change some assumptions of the CDS pricing market standard, we obtain different CDS prices. The differences in the CDS prices grow with an increase in time to maturity. It can clearly been stated that no singular, "correct" pricing method exists.

Generally, it seems that more market data input lead to more solid CDS prices and a more realistic modelling of the PD and especially the behaviour to the PD against the time to maturity. The disadvantages of those approaches, demanding more market data are a longer computational time and concerns regarding the quality of the market data for each maturity. Such concerns, especially with respect to the liquidity between different maturities, always remain. In contrary, simple approaches such as a constant hazard rate also lead faster to acceptable results. As far as the problem of the maturity of market data is concerned, the best solution according to our research is to interpolate between different maturities. The determination and construction of the discounting curve has a major impact, especially for CDS contracts with longer maturities. In particular, the discounting curve strongly influences the implied PD and the choice of the discounting interest rate curve is of particular interest if a central counterparty comes into play.

We discovered that, according to our data, the iTraxx Europe series 15 is not 100 % replicable by its members for any of the applied pricing models. Additionally, our research shows that there is a difference in liquidity between CDS index market quotes and single-name CDS market quotes.

In the second paper of this dissertation, we derived our own risk benchmark, which we call the "strike of default" (SOD). We determined the SOD through cross-sectional pricing between the credit market and the option market, obviously considering the same underlying. The idea of the SOD is to combine the implied PD from both markets to get a time-depending share price, at which the markets believe the underlying will default. By means of CDS and option pricing methods, we are able to determine the SOD for any exchange-listed company, where option

M. Schmidt, *Pricing and Liquidity of Complex and Structured Derivatives*, SpringerBriefs in Finance, DOI 10.1007/978-3-319-45970-7_5

and CDS market data are available. Our concept and construction of the SOD as well as the SOD's behaviour seems plausible, according to our research.

Unfortunately, we cannot hold our presumption that the SOD also is a suitable tool to compare the risk profile of different companies. A lower SOD does not necessarily imply that the company is more unlikely to default than a company with a higher SOD. This behaviour is caused by the structure of the implied volatility surface. Nevertheless, the implied probability of default is good additional information to the SOD for the purpose of comparison on risk profiles of two companies. Further, in some cases we observe a rise of the SOD with increasing time to maturity. Even though this behaviour can be quantitatively explained, it does not make any economic sense. The reason for this phenomenon is the quality of the market data, and the volatility surface for DOOM put options in particular. Our back-test, using different approaches on the determination of the applied volatility, also shows the same incidence, which supports our basic approach. In the case of a higher SOD for longer maturities we suggest assuming a constant SOD for all maturities, with the biggest—therefore the most conservative approach—SOD value available. Furthermore, we are able to construct a SOD function, predicting the SOD for maturities that are not available as grid points.

In the third paper, we analysed the SOD's sensitivities towards their most important input parameters, the implied volatility surface and the CDS spreads. Our finding is that the SOD seems to be time-independent to impacts on changes in the input parameters. Especially, changes in the CDS spread are only important, if the CDS deal spread changes simultaneously. The sensitivity towards the implied volatility surfaces is negligible, but we have to admit that the investigated changes are rather minor in comparison to the absolute value of the applied volatilities.

In the first part of the time series study, we examined whether the SOD theory holds, i.e. that the company defaults if the company's share price reaches the SOD. During our observation period of almost three years (from 2013-20-21 to 2015-12-22), only two companies (Commerzbank and RWE) should have defaulted. There are several reasons why those companies did not default according to the SOD theory. In case of the Commerzbank, the most obvious reason was that the German government is a stakeholder of the bank. For RWE the reason was the German government's decision to withdraw from nuclear power due to the nuclear catastrophe of Fukushima. Nevertheless, both companies are part of industries that are regulated by the government, and therefore these companies will most certainly be kept alive by the government if a bankruptcy might be impending.

In the second part of the time series study, we examined whether the SOD can explain or predict the performance of the corresponding company. In general, we must admit that the explanatory power of the SOD for the future performance of the company is rather weak. Nevertheless, for one or especially two-year performances, the longer SODs (one-year or even two-year) seems to have some influence (R^2-values between 11 and 18 %) on the predictability respectively explanation of the performance. The regressions on the other hand always seem to be heteroscedastic, which reduce the interpretation of those regressions. The enhancement of the regulation indicator improves the explanatory power of the regression. The regulation indication and the SOD always have a negative coefficient meaning that the performance tends to be better, if the SOD is low and the company is not regulated.

Due to all these facts and studies, we strongly believe that the SOD is an extremely flexible risk measure. The research shows that the assumptions hold, even though this risk measure is rather theoretical. Most importantly, the SOD is based purely on market data, which is a big advantage from our point of view, since the SOD is not reliant on only occasionally available balance sheet data. The historical data show that SOD predicted defaults in the past, but fortunately no default occurred. These examples of Commerzbank and RWE can be explained due to their particular circumstances. However, there is nothing wrong with a risk measure being too conservative and being too sensitive towards defaults. In case of the opposite, we would be worried. Even if the SOD theory reveals some weaknesses and boundaries, we believe that the general idea of cross-sectional pricing, i.e. the comprehension of all available market data, is the key for understanding and examination of risks concerning companies, countries or the financial market in general.

Appendix

A.1 Influence of Industrial Sub-index on the iTraxx Europe

In this section we take a look at the different industries of the iTraxx Europe series 15. All its members are divided into five different industries namely auto & industry, consumer, energy, financial and TMT (technology, media and telecommunication). We investigate whether there is one industry that affects the index more or less than other industries. Since these industrial sub-indices are not equally weighted, we assume that the influence of each sub-index is close to its weight in the index. We apply a linear regression on the performance of the index as well as on the performance of the industrial sub-indices. We use the same dataset as in the previous section, i.e. the dataset described in Sect. 2.5. This time we only use dates, where all member quotes are available. Therefore, we have 239 dates of observations instead of 242 dates as before.

A.1.1 Methodology

In order to gain proper prices from the market spreads, we calculated a CDS price for each day and each member and a price for each industry-index as the mean over all member prices of that particular sub-index. For reasons of simplicity we apply a constant hazard rate structure, as explained in Sect. 2.3, the single curve approach, as explained in Sect. 2.4, and we interpolate linearly between constant maturity CDS market data, as explained in Sect. 2.5. We also determine the index price based on the member prices i.e. as the mean over all members prices and compare this reproduced index price to market index price. As expected theses prices are not the same and these different prices could be interpreted as a lack of liquidity between the index quotes and the member quotes. Nevertheless, the data show that the reproduced indices prices and the indices prices are highly correlated. The correlations are 0.996 for the three-year index, 0.992 for the five-year index, 0.99 for the seven-year index and for 0.979 the ten-year index. Then we derive for each

M. Schmidt, *Pricing and Liquidity of Complex and Structured Derivatives*,
SpringerBriefs in Finance, DOI 10.1007/978-3-319-45970-7

day the daily performance for each industrial sub-index as well as for the index (original and reproduced) and for each maturity. In other words we calculate a time series of 239 performances per index. We reproduce index and each industrial-sub index.

Our goal is to compare the index movements ξ to the movements of the industrial sub-sectors $(x_1, \ldots, x_5)$. Furthermore, we would like to check the performance of the reproduced index $\overline{\xi}$ with the performances of the sub-indices. Since we apply a linear regression the model would look like this

$$\xi_l = b_{0,l} + \sum_{i=1}^{5} b_{i,l} x_{i,l}$$

with $l \in (3, 5, 7, 10)$ representing the different maturities, ξ_l the performance of the index, $b_{0,l}$ is the intercept and $x_{1,l}$ is the parameter for the auto & industrial industry with its coefficient $b_{1,l}$, $x_{2.l}$ is the parameter for the consumer industry with its coefficient $b_{2,l}$, $x_{3,l}$ is the parameter for the energy industry with its coefficient $b_{3,l}$, $x_{4,l}$ is the parameter for the financial industry with its coefficient $b_{4,l}$ and x_5 being the parameter for the TMT industry with its coefficient $b_{5,l}$. This model is identified with 233 degrees of freedom, we have 239 equations with six variables, and the sub-industries are not equally distributed. This means, that in the case of the iTraxx Europe series 15, we have 30 companies in the auto & industry sub-index and in the consumer sub-index (24 %), 25 companies in finance sub-index (20 %) and 20 in the energy and TMT sub-index (16 %). Therefore, we assume that the industries influence the index with their overall weight, i.e. the parameter would be around 0.24, 0.2 and 0.16. This same model is applied to the reproduced index as well as to the original index price to gain a feeling of the lack of liquidity between the index and its members.

A.1.2 Results

The results of these regressions are listed in the following tables. First, each regression possesses a high R^2, as we observe in Table A.1. That result is not surprising since the index consists out of these sub-indices and that is also a reason for the very small intercepts of the regressions. Secondly, there is no particular trend in these results, i.e. none of these parameters are relatively constant. The parameters differ strongly from our intuitive assumption that the parameters are close to the weight of the sub-index.

Nevertheless, there are some parameters that are worth to mention for the regression on the original index, as Table A.1 shows. For the shorter maturities of three respectively five years, the financial sub-index owns a rather strong leverage on the index. About 50 % of the performance of the sub-index influence the overall index, e.g. if the financial index gains about 10 % per day the index rises about

Table A.1 The results of the regression on the original index with the parameters for each sub-index, their intercept and the R^2 are shown

Industry	3 years (b_i) (n = 239)	5 years (b_i) (n = 239)	7 years (b_i) (n = 239)	10 years (b_i) (n = 239)
Auto & Industry	0.208	0.307	0.311	0.155
Consumer	0.181	0.172	0.189	0.116
Energy	0.192	0.041	−0.062	0.177
Financial	0.546	0.470	0.277	0.230
TMT	0.056	0.128	0.243	0.303
Intercept	0.000	0.000	0.000	0.000
R^2	0.809	0.815	0.762	0.736

5 %. For the longer maturities the influence by the financial sub-index decreases. For the seven-year maturity the energy sub-index even has a negative influence on the index. As mentioned earlier, we also derive the regression for the reproduced index. These results are listed in Table A.2.

Since the values of the reproduced index are based on the members, it does not surprise that the parameter R^2 is equal to one, meaning the replicated index is fully explained by the sub-indices. Correspondingly, the intercepts have to be zero. The differences between the R^2 can be seen as the unexplained ratio due to the lack of liquidity, which rises with longer maturities. O'Kane (2011) observed the same result, i.e. the lack of liquidity rises with the maturity. The parameters for the reproduced indices differ a lot from the parameters based on the original index values, which can also be due to the liquidity lack. The parameters for the reproduced index are nearly constant over all maturities and the energy sub-index even meets our assumption that the parameters are close to the weight of the sub-index. The financial sub-index is not as dominant in the shorter maturities as in the original index regression, but its influence is greater that its actual weight. The auto & industry sub-index as well as the consumer index have a smaller empirical influence on the replicated index than their actual weight.

Table A.2 The results of the regression on the reproduced index with the parameters for each sub-index, their intercept and the explaining parameter R^2 are shown

Industry	3 years (n = 239)	5 years (n = 239)	7 years (n = 239)	10 years (n = 239)
Auto & Ind.	0.161	0.161	0.161	0.160
Consumer	0.197	0.194	0.192	0.190
Energy	0.160	0.162	0.161	0.162
Financial	0.242	0.244	0.245	0.247
TMT	0.240	0.239	0.240	0.240
Intercept	0.000	0.000	0.000	0.000
R^2	1.000	1.000	1.000	1.000
ΔR^2	0.191	0.185	0.238	0.264

Table A.3 For each maturity, the t-statistics of the parameters for the original index and their p-values in brackets are shown

Industry	3 years (n = 239)	5 years (n = 239)	7 years (n = 239)	10 years (n = 239)
Auto & Ind.	2.080 (0.019)	2.600 (0.005)	2.352 (0.010)	1.256 (0.105)
Consumer	5.683 (0.000)	4.803 (0.000)	4.723 (0.000)	2.620 (0.005)
Energy	2.217 (0.014)	0.405 (0.343)	−0.547 (0.708)	1.527 (0.064)
Financial	4.342 (0.000)	2.974 (0.002)	1.596 (0.056)	1.459 (0.073)
TMT	1.429 (0.077)	1.272 (0.102)	2.147 (0.016)	2.675 (0.004)

Last but not least we want to take a look at the t-statistics and the p-values of the parameters gained from the original index. These parameters are shown in Table A.3. The t-statistics for the reproduced index are all fine, i.e. all parameters are significant. The p-value represents the quantile of the student t distribution with 233 degrees of freedom as it is the case in our regression. The smaller the p-value, the more reliable are the calculated parameters.

The high parameters of the financial sub-index for shorter maturities are very significant according to the t-statistic, but the seven-year parameter for the energy sub-index is not reliable at all. For the consumer industry all parameters seem to be quiet suitable.

A.1.3 Conclusion

The results show that there are no particular patterns in the influence of the industrial sub-indices, in terms of one sub-index having a higher weight on the index movement, over all maturities. Nevertheless, for the shorter maturities the financial sub-index seems to contain a major role. Due to the lack of liquidity and the quality of the CDS market data, an unexplained doubt concerning the significance and the reliability of the derived parameters still exist. The primary assumption that the sub-index influence is close to the weight of the sub-index can be rejected.

A.2 Investment/Hedging Strategy Based on the SOD

Based on our findings on the time series analysis of the SOD, we set up a hedging experiment, where we take a look at a certain trading strategy based on our time series analysis. We show that based on historical data, we are able to yield at least

5 % in 9 months, 9.2 % in 15 months and 31 % in 27 months with a reasonable risk. Since stock price and options rely on the firm's equity capital and the CDS on the company's debt, finding a wining investment strategy could be seen as equity-debt arbitrage. We assume that the credit risk based on equity and the credit risk based on the debts should be equal in an efficient market. That is because of the presumption that if one defaults, the other one automatically defaults as well.

A.2.1 Methodology

We would like to investigate how to hedge a CDS protection sells with American put options according to the SOD. The SOD is determined by digital American options with a deep-out-of-the-money (DOOM) strike. Such specific options practically do not exist in the markets, or if they do, they do not possess a high degree of liquidity. Therefore, we have to consider American put options, which are available on the market and, depending on the underlying, are very liquid. We hope to find a strategy from a CDS protection seller perspective, including the costs and income from the CDS deal, which lead to earnings and a partially hedge against a default of the company. If the company does not default and the share price drops below the strike, we also achieve some earnings. In Fig. A.1 we see, that with a two-year SOD of 0.24 and a put option at 0.7, it is possible to gain a profit of about 0.1*(spot at 2011-03-21) at maturity.

We calculate theoretical option prices instead of using market prices for two reasons. First, it is not guaranteed to find options with the exact maturity or strike as needed. Secondly, in that case we would have to interpolate between the market prices. Such interpolation between market prices is not necessarily better than use of an interpolated volatility from an implied volatility surface. For the deviation of the American put option price, we apply the Crank-Nicolson method like we did the

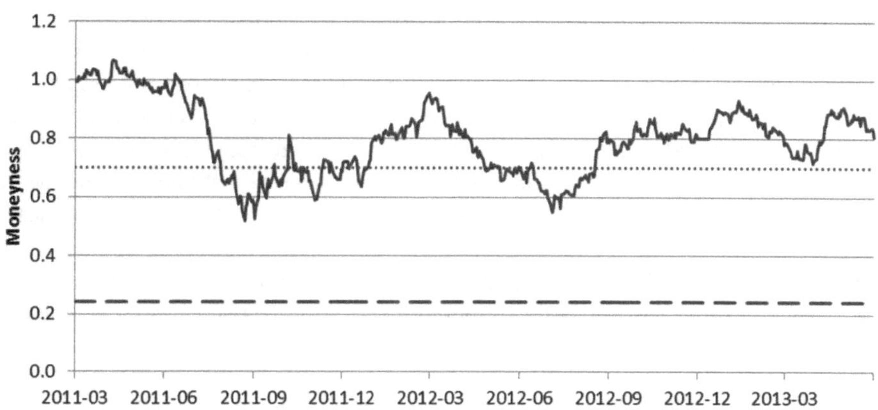

Fig. A.1 The performance of the Deutsche Bank share starting at 2011-03-21 with the calculated two-year SOD at 0.24 and a possible option strike at 0.7

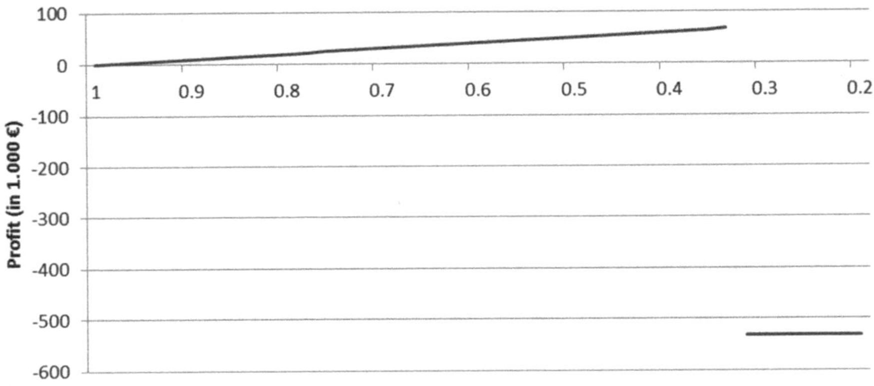

Fig. A.2 The profit (in 1.000€) at maturity with 1.000 put options with strike at moneyness one (with spot = 100€) and a SOD of 0.32 and a nominal of 1.000.000€ for the CDS

SOD calculation. Also like in the SOD determination, we assume the dividend to be null due to the fact that we are only interested in the decrease of the stock price, i.e. we assume the company is not able to pay any dividends.[1] Furthermore, we calculate the option prices where we apply a strike of 1, 0.95, 0.9 and so on until the last step before the SOD.

Another interesting question for us is the possibility of earnings without investing any money. From a CDS protection seller perspective—we do not differentiate whether it is a short sell or not—the CDS is comparable to a bond without the payment of the nominal, unless the company defaults, since the protection seller gathers regular fixed payments. What if the protection seller uses these earnings to buy American put options on the same company. If the share drops, the protection seller gains a profit, unless the company defaults, which we assume to happen when the strike price reaches the SOD. In this paper we distinguish between the earnings one might achieve at the opening of the CDS contract,[2] which we refer to as earnings "at date", and the additional earnings due to coupon payments, which we will call earnings "in total" (all coupon payments and the earnings at the beginning of the contract). In our data set we calculate the SOD at CDS coupon dates, i.e. with no accrued interest, which means positive earnings at date are equivalent to the CDS market spread being higher than the contractual spread. In Fig. A.2 we observe the profit at maturity of 1000 put options with a strike of one in moneyness, a CDS on the nominal of 1,000,000€ and an SOD of 0.32 in terms of moneyness.

Until the share drops below the SOD, where we believe the company defaults, we are able to gain a profit of $(strike - spot) * number_{options}$. In case of a default, the protection seller has to pay the amount of $(1 - R) * Nominal$, which is reduced

[1]Therefore are our option price more theoretical and not directly from the market.

[2]If the market spread is higher than the contractual spread and the accrued interests are not of any problem, the CDS price will not be zero and the protection buyer must pay the protection seller a certain amount to open the CDS contract.

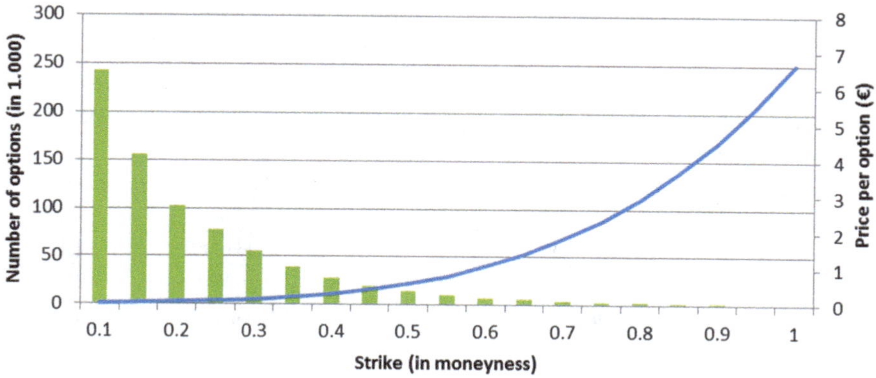

Fig. A.3 The average price of an option with regard to its strike and the number of options that can be bought with about €8140 (the average available money over all maturities, if we assume all earnings i.e. at the opening of the contract plus all future coupon payments)

by the payment for the option, anyway. In our example, hitting the SOD leads to a payment of €600,000 and to earnings from the options of €72,000, i.e. leaving €528,000 to be paid by the protection seller. However, the payment without the options would have been higher. If we only invest the earnings at the opening of the contract, such amount would be smaller than the investment of all future coupon payments. Of course, the more options we buy, the more we earn once the options are in-the-money and the CDS does not default. In Fig. A.3 we see the linkage between option price and the number of options, which we are able to obtain with the same amount. In our last part, we analyse portfolios in which we theoretically sold CDS protections and bought American put options with the same maturity as well as a strike of one in terms of moneyness, i.e. options which are at the money. We differ between a portfolio including companies with a positive earnings at date, in which we invest all these earnings directly into these options on the one hand, and a portfolio consisting of all companies with a positive earning in total, in which we invest this amount into the options even if we do not possess the money at that time on the other hand.

A.2.2 Results

As outlined above, we derived option prices for each pricing date, underlying and runtime with decreasing strikes (in steps of 0.05 in terms of moneyness) until the last step before the SOD is reached. We want to discuss the "optimal" strike of the American put option either with regards to the best hedge, i.e. the highest pay out if the SOD has been reached, or with regard to the maximum profit that could have been reached, i.e. the highest pay-out possible in the lifetime of the put option. We distinguish between the available money to invest. Either we invest only the earnings gathered from opening the CDS contract, which we refer to as the money

Table A.4 The comparison between the optimal strike regarding the maximum profit respectively and the best hedge at default of money "at date" are shown

At date	Strike	Earnings	SOD	PD (%)	E (paym.)	Profit (best)	Profit (last)
6 M (max)	0.94	1433.40	0.34	0.41	2396.52	3886.90	255.97
1 Y (max)	0.94	1783.15	0.31	0.75	4390.56	4185.94	1486.96
2 Y (max)	0.96	2584.52	0.27	1.67	9761.11	3266.95	1258.40
6 M (SoD)	0.38	1433.40	0.34	0.41	1740.85	1938.59	0.00
1 Y (SoD)	0.36	1783.15	0.31	0.75	3613.93	2314.56	1319.41
2 Y (SoD)	0.33	2584.52	0.27	1.67	8507.51	625.56	580.00

All values are averages where the 6 months values are based on 144 observations, the 12 months on 136 observations and the 24 months on 108 observations (the vary because not all deals are positive on the pricing date)

"at date", or we also invest directly all future coupon payments, what we call money "in total". Table A.4 displays our aggregated results concerning the optimal moneyness with regard to the maximum profits that are labelled with "(max)" in the first three lines.

The optimal moneyness with regard to the maximum pay-out in case of default, i.e. at SOD or lower, are labelled with "(SOD)" and are represented in the last three lines. The maximum possible profit, labelled as "profit (best)", is derived from the opening date of the CDS contract until maturity or the last date of our data, which ever may come first.[3] Similarly the last profit, labelled as "profit (last)", either is the profit calculated with the share price at maturity or at the last date of our data. In this table we only consider contracts, in which the protection seller would gain an amount at CDS opening that we would invest directly into different put options. The average money invested is shown in the third column and increases with the maturity since the spreads are usually higher for longer maturities. If we are looking for the maximisation of profit, we can see that the optimal strike of the American put options (in the second column) at about 0.95 (in terms of moneyness) is almost the same for all maturities. This result might be expected, since the difference between executed asset prices and strike is very high, but the number of options is smaller since the option price is higher. This relation between option price and number of options is mirrored Fig. A.3. The average SOD is decreasing and the average probability of default is increasing with a longer maturity. These effects have already been observed and explained in Schmidt (2014a, b, c). The results outlined above are another affirmation of our assumption. We calculated the expectation of the payment of default, the sixth column in the table, as follows

$$pd * \left[(1 - R) * \text{nominal} - (\text{strike} - \text{SOD}) * \text{spot} * \text{num}_{\text{options}}\right]$$

[3]Our very last date of end of day quotes is the 2013-10-14.

where pd is the probability of default, R is the recovery rate, SOD is measured in moneyness, spot is the stock price at CDS opening and $num_{options}$ is the number of options. Since we assume a constant recovery rate of 40 %, all the parameters are known at the opening of the contract since we assume a default only to occur when the SOD barrier is hit. We derive the pd hazard rate, which we extract from the market quote, and use the formula that we discussed earlier. The average expected value of the payment at default is increasing with time, which probably is an intuitive thought, since the probability of default rises, even if SOD falls. The last two columns are the average profits that are possible at best. In such scenario the protection seller would execute the option at the lowest share price and the profit at the last date, i.e. decide to hold the options until maturity. These profits are adjusted by the earning of the deal i.e. these are earnings on top of the earnings of the CDS contract. If we now compare the results of the strike of the maximum profit to the results of the maximum protection in the default event, we notice that the average strike drops from 0.95 to a range from 0.33 to 0.38. It is due to the construction of these results that the profit at best drops, but in comparison, the average of the expected value does not drop as much as we would expect. In other words, the expected payment is only reduced to 72 % for the six months contract (82 % for the one-year and 87 % to the two-year contract) on average, but the maximum profit is reduced to 50 % for the six months contract (49 % for the one-year and even 19 % for the two-year). This means the benefit of a higher payment in case of a credit event reduces the possible gains in a higher ratio than the raise of security. This impression is reinforced by the probability (or in our case the realized rates) of the option being not only in-the-money but also profitable. We find the rates of gaining a profit—look at Table A.5 for more information—are a lot higher, if we chose the strike of the option to be closer to one in terms of moneyness. That is not surprising, since we constructed the optimal strike in that particular way. However, the relation is rather astonishing. Nearly every second deal delivers a profit during its life span and, if we chose a strike at about 0.95, about 9 % of the options do so even at maturity. If, on the other hand, we chose a hedging strike maximum of payment at SOD, the percentage of being profitable drops to about 1 % or even below.

Table A.5 The comparison between the optimal strike regarding the maximum profit respectively and the best hedge at default on money invested "in total" are shown

In total	Strike	Earnings	SOD	PD (%)	E (paym.)	Profit (best)	Profit (last)
6 M (max)	0.93	4344.04	0.32	0.75	4088.28	11,265.61	1390.26
1 Y (max)	0.94	7033.15	0.29	1.23	6512.13	18,271.03	6058.25
2 Y (max)	0.96	13,135.72	0.24	2.82	14,846.54	23,378.31	10,337.13
6 M (SoD)	0.37	4344.04	0.32	0.75	1508.57	4340.73	269.00
1 Y (SoD)	0.34	7033.15	0.29	1.23	2525.66	9516.12	5169.32
2 Y (SoD)	0.3	13,135.72	0.24	2.82	6850.27	9627.00	6326.16

All values are averages where the 6 months values are based on 185 observations, the 12 months on 179 observations and the 24 months on 180 observations (the vary because not all deals are positive "in total")

Table A.6 These are the hit percentage of profits due to their kind of investment and in terms of optimal strike for the hedging option

At date				In total			
Max		SOD		Max		SOD	
% B-Profit (%)	% L-Profit (%)	% B-Profit (%)	% L-Profit (%)	% B-Profit (%)	% L-Profit (%)	% B-Profit (%)	% L-Profit (%)
60.42	11.11	0.69	0.00	56.76	10.81	1.62	0.54
52.94	8.82	1.47	0.74	51.40	8.94	1.68	0.56
47.22	8.33	0.93	0.93	43.89	5.56	1.67	0.56

In Table A.6 we gathered the same information as in Table A.5, but this time we did not only invest the earnings at the beginning of the contract but also all the future coupon earnings, i.e. we are optimistic that the underlying does not default until maturity. Of course there is a risk involved that not all coupons will be paid, but if the company defaults the payments will be a lot higher than some missing coupons and the options will in any case cover at least the loss due to outstanding coupon payments. Here, we also include contracts where we have negative earnings at the opening of the contract i.e. were the protection seller has to pay an amount to the protection buyer to enter into the contract but with positive earnings until maturity. The results are very similar to the earlier ones discussed earlier. The average strike for the "maximisation" of profit again is very high at about 0.95 and the profit "at best" is a lot higher than in the "at date" case[4] whereas the expected payment at default does not equally increase. This time the relation between the maximization and the security is not as dramatic as earlier. The reduction of the expected payments is about the same ratio as the best possible profit. For example, if we look at the six months maturity, the expected payment is reduced to 37 % (from 4088.28 to 1508.57), which is close to a cutback to 39 % (from 11,265.61 to 4340.73) at the best possible profit. Nevertheless, the probability of gaining a profit is quite similar as in the "at date" case. It drops from about 44–57 to 2 %, respectively from 5–11 % to below 1 %. The conclusion from our thoughts is to buy American put options with a strike close to the current spot in order to most likely obtain profits without the SOD being hit. Furthermore, it has been shown by the data that it is better to invest the amount of all future payments i.e. to invest some own money at opening in the options, because if the company does default before maturity, on average the higher number of options compiles a higher profit than the loss of the coupon payments.

Until now we have only looked at the hedging of a single CDS contract. Therefor we would like to take a look at possible portfolios, in which we sell CDS protections and invest the earnings in at-the-money (ATM) American put options, i.e. with a strike of one in terms of moneyness. As mentioned earlier, we differ between two portfolios investing either the earnings at the opening of the contract or additionally all future coupons. Furthermore, we only consider CDS contracts

[4]The leverage varies between 2.8 and 7.2.

from our data set, which are terminated until our last observation date. In Table A.7 we find such portfolios in which all the money is invested with positive earnings at the beginning of the CDS contracts. The first column shows the date of the opening contract, the second one shows the maturity of the products, the third column lists the number of companies[5] in this portfolio and the forth column tells us the average number of options per company in that particular portfolio. The fifth column is the sum of the best executions of the options assuming that the American option has been executed at the best possible moment. If, on the other hand, the protection seller wants to hold the option until maturity in case of a credit event, that outcome is figured in the sixth column. Apart from a few exceptions the profits are higher—both at best and at last—the longer the maturity. This is not surprising since we generally hold more options the longer their maturity. The number of options increases the leverage and the longer maturity makes it more likely that a lower share price is reached. The last columns deal with the risk of each portfolio. It is not trivial to calculate a value at risk (VaR) for these portfolios since they do not only consist out of options but also of CDS contracts. Therefore we decided to treat theses portfolios as if they included only shares. Meaning for each contract we said that the amount of

$$\text{nominal} * (1 - \text{R}) - (\text{strike} - \text{SOD}) * \text{spot} * \text{number}_{\text{options}}$$

is at risk. We apply the used volatility, the historic correlation matrix and the standard assumption, that asset returns are normally distributed, and calculated the VaR to the 95 and 99 % level until maturity. This deviation of the VaR is not ideal. It overestimates the risk, because our portfolio does not exist of shares only. Also, it is not as sensible to smaller changes in the share price. Our portfolios are very sensitive to large or even extreme downward movements of the share price. Therefore, it might be interesting for future research to apply a fat tails. Nevertheless, our VaR determination does give us some idea of the risk. The last column is the sum of the expected payments, i.e. term above times the probability of default. This value does not consider any correlations and therefore is not a proper value either but gives some kind of lower risk barrier. There were no claims in any portfolio, i.e. no credit event happened, even though some SODs were hit. As we would expect, the VaR rises, the longer the portfolio lasts. However, the more companies are contained in a portfolio the less the risk increases with an additional member. This effect is of course known as diversification. The construction of Table A.8 is the same as in Table A.7, but this time we invested also all future coupon payments in the ATM American put options and included all companies with positive earnings until maturity. Thus, the leverage is bigger since the protection seller is able to buy more options and the average profits are a lot higher than in the "at date" case. The average profits increase at least by the factor four whereas the risk only rises by about 10–27 % in the VaR. In the second case

[5]For each company we sell a CDS protection and buy several ATM American put options.

Table A.7 This tables shows the terminated synthetic portfolios with only the earnings invested into put options from the selling of the CDS protection

Valuation date	Runtime	#Members	#Options	Profit at best	Profit at maturity	95 % VaR	99 % VaR	E (payment at default)
2011-03-21	0.5	18	352	65,101.45	37,064.90	1,161,987.22	1,650,872.08	36,606.63
2011-06-20	0.5	17	421	76,974.70	13,478.29	1,111,832.82	1,579,616.15	38,184.52
2011-09-20	0.5	6	255	7502.30	3880.19	842,335.15	1,196,732.26	33,588.70
2011-12-20	0.5	10	527	12,348.49	5580.92	924,163.71	1,312,988.68	52,465.31
2012-03-20	0.5	19	498	61,167.75	17,107.77	1,295,497.11	1,840,553.83	38,088.46
2012-06-20	0.5	11	275	10,051.78	1676.64	913,179.73	1,297,383.39	34,172.79
2012-09-20	0.5	21	536	30,408.02	15,238.56	1,299,429.60	1,846,140.84	46,781.15
2011-03-21	1	18	431	93,736.73	46,944.69	1,170,141.76	1,662,457.51	76,854.48
2011-06-20	1	18	575	108,372.81	25,790.80	1,172,099.29	1,665,238.63	89,520.59
2011-09-20	1	3	101	2666.86	0.00	652,656.72	927,250.09	33,954.22
2011-12-20	1	9	180	5467.40	0.00	1,018,204.44	1,446,595.33	81,061.13
2012-03-20	1	19	324	43,664.28	15,521.48	1,344,089.58	1,909,590.68	79,760.44
2012-06-20	1	10	750	14,756.22	5345.38	839,713.15	1,193,007.10	58,443.85
2011-03-21	2	18	689	122,963.30	62,129.31	1,122,932.17	1,595,385.34	186,804.87
2011-06-20	2	15	476	83,997.95	26,493.32	1,002,928.38	1,424,892.14	156,991.36

The VaR are calculated until maturity and the expected payments are just the sum of the positions, i.e. no correlations applied

Table A.8 Terminated synthetic portfolios where the earnings at the beginning and all coupons are positive ("total") are invested into put options from the selling of the CDS protection

Valuation date	Runtime	#Members	#Options	Profit at best	Profit at maturity	95 % VaR	99 % VaR	E (payment at default)
2011-03-21	0.5	22	979	239,653.19	139,830.85	1,293,617.54	1,837,883.45	65,242.48
2011-06-20	0.5	22	1486	315,156.87	74,927.85	1,264,089.21	1,795,931.62	73,098.06
2011-09-20	0.5	16	1725	69,300.17	20,734.60	1,544,438.51	2,194,232.76	170,803.76
2011-12-20	0.5	19	3855	93,678.32	32,211.79	1,474,595.34	2,095,004.35	184,478.41
2012-03-20	0.5	22	1276	183,884.28	51,159.69	1,416,553.37	2,012,542.29	65,971.93
2012-06-20	0.5	18	1211	46,297.43	8290.05	1,325,610.02	1,883,336.19	88,193.03
2012-09-20	0.5	22	1557	100,522.30	54,329.92	1,300,674.49	1,847,909.49	50,451.06
2011-03-21	1	22	1955	494,753.05	274,402.72	1,259,609.91	1,789,567.74	114,137.02
2011-06-20	1	22	2052	499,777.08	138,906.59	1,249,277.38	1,774,887.99	136,909.08
2011-09-20	1	16	2240	117,426.90	23,455.89	1,355,854.89	1,926,306.04	271,254.72
2011-12-20	1	17	4068	84,921.17	25,706.38	1,322,712.66	1,879,219.81	212,440.29
2012-03-20	1	20	1369	199,195.37	77,376.39	1,333,880.53	1,895,086.36	85,961.08
2012-06-20	1	16	2103	84,329.33	25,908.48	1,130,140.02	1,605,625.77	127,862.86
2011-03-21	2	22	3095	847,437.54	418,488.42	1,209,497.67	1,718,371.69	282,828.02
2011-06-20	2	21	2973	776,379.70	274,601.34	1,159,982.38	1,648,023.75	275,861.36

The VaR are calculated until maturity and the expected payments are just the sum of the positions, i.e. no correlations applied

are also profits guaranteed even if the options are to be hold until maturity. It seems in the "in total" case, where a lot more members are involved in each portfolio, that the VaRs are more or less equal, even if they are calculated over different time horizons. This means the risk is decreasing with time while the average profits are increasing. It seems that a portfolio with a higher number of options seems to obtain a good profit with a moderate risk, since we did not invest any money on our own.

Based on our last results we came up with the following investment strategy. This time we invest some money, whereas before we only considered investing money that we gathered from the CDS protection sells. The idea is to sell CDS protections again, but this time we invest the amount of all future payments and invest a risk cushion that will help if a credit event occurs. Then we invest all profits from the CDS openings plus the amount of all future coupon payments again into ATM American options. The risk cushion is invested at risk-free rate so that in a credit event the money is directly available. Until maturity we gather the coupon payments plus the earnings from an (early) execution of the options if any. Furthermore at maturity we gained the risk cushion plus the risk-free interest back. Now we are able to derive a range of performance for our portfolios. Holding the options until maturity builds the lower limit of the performance range whereas the best execution of the options possible builds the upper performance limit. For the risk cushion we use the 95 % VaR, the 99 % VaR or the size of the payment, if one company does default i.e. €600,000. These results are placed in Table A.9. The performance ranges are the higher, the lower the risk cushion. This is because the earnings, apart from the risk-free earnings, are the same, but the investment is lower. The performance until maturity for the six months varies between 5 % up to 59.2 %. In times of the low risk-free rates this is a tremendous success. We can say that the longer the maturity, the higher the performances. For one-year contracts the range is between 9.2 and 88.1 %. For the two-year contracts the performance varies from 31 to even 129.2 %. The upper limits of all portfolio performance will probably never be realized since it is utopic to execute all options at the best possible time. The risk of the portfolios is a lot lower. In each portfolio, one credit event is at least possible and for a higher risk cushion, up to three defaults is prevented. A counterparty risk does not exist. If the counter part of the CDS defaults, so does the contract, i.e. our risk of default of the underlying of this CDS evaporated. The biggest risk is that several underlyings collapse, which can be reduced if the portfolio manager sells the CDS protections or buys a CDS protection—to this point, we consistently assumed a passive behaviour of the portfolio manager.

A.2.3 Conclusion

When it comes to partially hedging a possible credit default with American put options that are paid via the CDS earnings, according to our findings, the best way to do so is to buy options with a strike close to spot at the opening of the CDS contract. We would assume it is better use a lower strike in order to buy more

Table A.9 The performance of portfolios where we invest a risk cushion, with the size of the VaR 95, VaR 99 or the amount of one default (600,000€) in our case, plus all future coupons

Valuation date	Runtime	#Members	Investment (95 %)	Investment (99 %)	Investment (1 D)	Perf. (95) (%)	Perf. (99) (%)	Perf. (1 D) (%)
2011-03-21	0.5	22	1,350,701.18	1,894,966.18	657,083.18	16.3–23.6	12.1–17.4	31.6–46.8
2011-06-20	0.5	22	1,332,588.85	1,864,431.85	668,499.85	12.6–30.7	9.6–22.5	23.2–59.2
2011-09-20	0.5	16	1,650,994.40	2,300,788.40	706,555.40	9.5–12.4	7.3–9.5	19.6–26.5
2011-12-20	0.5	19	1,639,803.88	2,260,212.88	765,208.88	13.7–17.4	10.4–13.2	27.2–35.3
2012-03-20	0.5	22	1,481,483.58	2,077,472.58	664,930.58	9.1–18.1	6.9–13.3	18.7–38.6
2012-06-20	0.5	18	1,395,755.51	1,953,481.51	670,145.51	6.6–9.4	5.1–7	12.7–18.3
2012-09-20	0.5	22	1,361,340.33	1,908,575.33	660,666.33	9–12.4	6.6–9	17.9–24.9
2011-03-21	1	22	1,383,380.40	1,913,338.40	723,770.40	30.6–46.6	22.7–34.2	56.7–87.1
2011-06-20	1	22	1,386,040.65	1,911,651.65	736,763.65	21.8–47.8	16.4–35.3	39.1–88.1
2011-09-20	1	16	1,546,271.00	2,116,722.00	790,416.00	15.4–21.5	11.7–16.1	28.4–40.3
2011-12-20	1	17	1,525,380.20	2,081,887.20	802,667.20	16.4–20.3	12.5–15.3	29.7–37.1
2012-03-20	1	20	1,429,089.00	1,990,294.00	695,208.00	13.4–21.9	10–16.1	26–43.5
2012-06-20	1	16	1,244,389.60	1,719,875.60	714,249.60	12.3–17	9.2–12.6	20.6–28.8
2011-03-21	2	22	1,506,330.88	2,015,204.88	896,832.88	49.4–77.9	37.5–58.8	81.4–129.2
2011-06-20	2	21	1,451,461.03	1,939,503.03	891,479.03	40.7–75.3	31–56.9	65–121.2

Then we invest the amount of the future coupon earnings plus the earnings at date into ATM American option and the risk cushion at the risk-free rate. Then we gain the CDS coupon over time, plus the risk free rate on the cushion plus the earnings from the options. The performance until maturity of these portfolios are shown in the last column, there are ranges where the lower boundary is the performance with the options hold until maturity and at the upper boundary the options are executed at the best possible moment

options, i.e. have a higher leverage on the earnings from the options and to have a higher payment at SOD or even lower, but it is very unlikely that these options ever gain a profit. Furthermore, we are able to gather a lot higher average profits if we also invest the money from future coupon payments.

There is a possible way to gain yields with a portfolio based on CDS protection sells and investing the earnings in ATM American put options. The longer the maturity is, the higher is the possible winnings. On the one hand, we are not completely sure how to measure the risk involved, but with our two risk measurements, the VaR and the sum of the expected payments, we tried to narrow the risk. We do not deny that better ways to measure the risk exist. Like in the case of a single CDS it is suggested by the data to invest all future coupons in ATM American puts, if we want to gather a high profit. It is particularly worth mentioning that in the case of the two-year maturities, it is possible that the profits are high enough to absorb one credit event. We demonstrated that, with our investment strategy, we are able to gain at least 5 % performance in nine months,[6] 9.2 % in 15 months or 31 % in 27 months with at least one credit event being saved.

As a future research topic, it could be interesting to discuss the subject of investing as much into the ATM American options, so that in the case of a default, the options produce enough earnings to cover the losses. We could also think of purchasing options with an European exercise style or down-and-in puts, which are not as expensive as American puts, i.e. able to gather more options and have similar effects.

[6]The maturity of a CDS contract is the runtime plus one coupon, i.e. three additionally months.

Literature

X. Burtshell, J. Gregory, J.-P. Laurent, A comparative analysis of CDO pricing models (2008)

B. Choros, W. Härdle, O. Okhrin, CDO and HAC (2009)

G. Danon, Pricing and Risk Analysis of correlation Products: Evidence of Synthetic CDO Swaps (2007a)

G.F. Danon, Pricing and risk analysis of correlation products: Evidence of synthetic CDO swaps. London Metropolitan University (2007b)

E.J. Elton, M.J. Gruber, D. Agrawal, C. Mann, Explaining the rate spread on corporate bonds. J. Finan. **56**(1), 247–277 (2001)

A. Eriksson, E. Ghysels, F. Wang, The normal inverse Gaussian distribution and the pricing of derivatives. J. Deriv. **16**(3), 23–37 (2009)

A.E. Greenberg, Tuning Correlation and Tail Risk to Market Prices of Liquid Tranches (2004)

A. Greenberg, R. Mashal, M. Naldi, L. Schloegl, Tuning correlation and tail risk to market prices of liquid tranches. Lehman Brothers quantitative credit research quarterly (2004)

M. Hofert, M. Scherer, CDO pricing with nested Archmidedean copulas. University of Ulm (2008)

J.C. Hull, A. White, Valuing credit default swaps I: No counterparty default risk. J. Deriv. **8**(1), 29–40 (2000)

J.C. Hull, A. White, Valuation of a CDO and an nth to default CDS without Monte Carlo simulation. J. Deriv. **12**(2), 8–32 (2004)

J.C. Hull, A. White, Valuing credit derivaties using an implied copula approach. J. Deriv. **14**(2), 8–28 (2006)

J.C. Hull, A. White, An improved implied copula model and its application to the valuation of bespoke CDO tranches. J Invesment Manag. **8**(3), 11–31 (2010)

J.C. Hull, A. White, LIBOR versus OIS: The derivatives discounting dilemma. J. Investment Manag. **11**(3), 14–27 (2012)

J.C. Hull, M. Predescu, A. White, The valuation of correlation-dependent credit derivatives using a structural model. J. Credit Risk **6**(3), 99–132 (2010)

J.-P. Laurent, J. Gregory, Basket default swaps, CDOs and factor copulas. J. Risk **7**(4), 103–122 (2005)

J.-P. Laurent, J. Gregory, X. Burtshell, A comparative analysis of CDO pricing models (2005)

D.X. Li, On default correlation: A copula fuction approach. Available at SSRN 187289 (1999)

A. McNeil, Sampling nested Archimedean copulas. J. Stat. Comput. Simul. **78**(6), 567–581 (2007)

D. O'Kane, Force-fitting CDS spreads to CDS index swaps. J. Deriv. **18**(3) (2011)

M.F. Schmidt, Credit default swaps from an equity point of view. *World Finance Conference* (2014a)

M.F. Schmidt, Different approaches on CDS valuation—an empirical study. *Unpublished working paper* (2014b)

M.F. Schmidt, Strike of default: Sensitivity and time series analysis. *Unpublished working paper* (2014c)

M. Schmidt, *Pricing and Liquidity of Complex and Structured Derivatives*,
SpringerBriefs in Finance, DOI 10.1007/978-3-319-45970-7

A. Veremyev, A. Nakonechnyi, S. Uryasev, R.T. Rockafeller, Implied copula CDO pricing model: entropy approach. Working paper (2009)

D. Wang, S.T. Rachev, F.J. Fabozzi, Pricing tranches of a CDO and a CDS index: recent advances and future research. In *Risk Assesment* (Physica, Karlsruhe, 2009), pp. 263–286

R. Zagst, S. Höchst, Pricing distressed CDOs with stochastic recovery. Rev. Deriv. Res. **13**(3), 219–244 (2010)

B.Z. Zhang, Explaining credit default swap spreads with equity volatility and jump risks of individual firms. Rev. Finan. Stud. **22**, 5099–5131 (2009)

FSC
www.fsc.org
MIX
Papier | Fördert
gute Waldnutzung
FSC® C083411

Kolibri 360 GmbH
Ferdinand-Jühlke-Straße 7
99095 Erfurt, Deutschland
produktsicherheit@kolibri360.de